"At low tide, the wind blowing across Spartina grass sounds like wind of the prairie. When the tide is in, the gentle music of moving water is added to the prairie rustle. . . ."

One of nature's greatest gifts is the string of salt marshes that edges the East Coast from Newfoundland to Florida—a ribbon of green growth, part solid land, part scurrying water. *Life and Death of the Salt Marsh* shows how these marshes are developed, what kinds of life inhabit them, how enormously they have contributed to man, and how ruthlessly man is destroying them.

"The Teals have done a thorough and impressive job. . . . The illustrations by Richard Fish are superb. They explain in pictures what words cannot convey. This book should produce a sense of outrage at the rape of nature and rally those who realize how fast our natural scene is disappearing beneath the bulldozer blade."

—*Newsday*

LIFE AND DEATH
OF THE SALT MARSH

John and Mildred Teal

Illustrated by Richard G. Fish

BALLANTINE BOOKS • NEW YORK

A condensed version of the first part of this book appeared in
the *Audubon Magazine*.

Library of Congress Catalog Card Number: 70-86614

ISBN 0-345-27093-2

This edition published by arrangement with Atlantic-Little,
Brown Books, in association with the Atlantic Monthly Press.

Manufactured in the United States of America

First Ballantine Books Edition: January 1971
Sixth Printing: January 1980

Cover photograph courtesy of Freelance Photographers Guild

To the Conservation Commission of the town of Fal-mouth, Massachusetts, and to other conservation-minded groups for their efforts in

PRESERVING SALT MARSHES

Preface

A book of this type is written only in part from the personal experiences of the authors. It depends on the work of others, laymen, scientists, and laboratories that have pursued an interest in one part or another of the complex of animals, plants, mud, and water that makes up salt marshes. To these unnamed people we are deeply indebted.

We have drawn heavily on the scientific work from the Sapelo Island Marine Institute of the University of Georgia, which provided us with a home laboratory and introduced us to salt marshes in 1955. Our thanks go to Dalhousie University in Halifax, Nova Scotia, which gave us the opportunity to work on the marshes of the Maritimes. Our thanks go also to the Woods Hole Oceanographic Institution, which has provided us with a base from which we did recent work as well as a collection of helpful colleagues who were able to fill in many gaps in our knowledge.

The staff of the Fish and Wildlife Service of the United States Department of the Interior has provided a great deal of helpful information about all aspects of salt marshes but especially about their conservation. Much of the data on the present status of conservation presented in the last chapter is taken from their records. The Audubon Society has been helpful with information on conservation.

Special mention must be made of several individuals who, pestered more than others, generously gave time and information. We thank A. C. Redfield, whose work on Barnstable Marsh provided information and inspiration, and who kindly read a portion of the manuscript; G. P. Spinner, who provided information on marsh conservation; R. H. Meade, who helped us gather geological information; and J. W. Kanwisher and David Masch, with whom we have worked in the marsh.

Even though many people contributed to the information and ideas presented in this book, the final interpretation of data must be charged to us. We alone are responsible for the errors that will come to light.

John and Mildred Teal

North Falmouth
June 1969

Contents

PART III

Marsh Conservation

LIFE *and* DEATH
of the
SALT MARSH

Introduction

ALONG THE EASTERN COAST OF NORTH AMERICA, from the north where ice packs grate upon the shore to the tropical mangrove swamps tenaciously holding the land together with a tangle of roots, lies a green ribbon of soft, salty, wet, low-lying land, the salt marshes.

The ribbon of green marshes, part solid land, part mobile water, has a definite but elusive border, now hidden, now exposed, as the tides of the Atlantic fluctuate. At one place and tide there is a line at which you can say, "Here begins the marsh." At another tide, the line, the "beginning of the marsh," is completely inundated and looks as though it had become part of the sea. The marsh reaches as far inland as the tides can creep and as far into the sea as marsh plants can find a roothold and live in saline waters.

The undisturbed salt marshes offer the inland visitor a series of unusual perceptions. At low tide, the wind blowing across *Spartina* grass sounds like wind on the prairie. When the tide is in, the gentle music of moving water is added to the prairie rustle. There are sounds of birds living in the marshes. The marsh wren advertises his presence with a reedy call, even at night, when most birds are still. The marsh hen, or clapper rail, calls in a loud, carrying cackle. You can hear the tiny, high-pitched rustling thunder of the herds of crabs moving through the grass as they flee before advancing feet or the more leisurely sound of movement they make on their daily migrations in search of food. At night, when the air is still and other sounds are quieted, an attentive listener can hear the bubbling of air from the sandy soil as a high tide floods the marsh.

The wetlands are filled with smells. They smell of the sea and salt water and of the edge of the sea, the sea with a little iodine and trace of dead life. The marshes smell of *Spartina*, a fairly strong odor mixed from the elements of sea and the smells of grasses. These are clean, fresh smells, smells that are pleasing to one who lives by the sea but strange and not altogether pleasant to one who has always lived inland.

Unfortunately, in marshes which have been disturbed, dug up, suffocated with loads of trash and fill, poisoned and eroded with the wastes from large cities, there is another smell. Sick marshes smell of hydrogen sulfide, a rotten egg odor. This odor is very faint in a healthy marsh.

As the sound and smell of the salt marsh are its own, so is its feel. Some of the marshes can be walked on, especially the landward parts. In the north, the *Spartina patens* marsh is covered with dense grass that may be cut for salt hay. Its roots bind the wet mud into a firm surface. But the footing is spongy on an unused hay marsh as the mat of other years' grass, hidden under the green growth, resists the walker's weight and springs back as he moves along.

In the southern marshes, only one grass covers the entire marsh area, *Spartina alterniflora*. On the higher parts of the marsh, near the land, the roots have developed into a mass that provides firm footing although the plants are much more separated than in the northern hay marshes and you squish gently on mud rather than grass. It is like walking on a huge trampoline. The ground is stiff. It is squishy and wet, to be sure, but still solid as you walk about. However, jump and you can feel the ground give under the impact and waves spread out in all directions. The ground is a mat of plant roots and mud on top of a more liquid layer underneath which gives slightly by flowing to all sides when you jump down on it.

As you walk toward the edge of the marsh, the seaward edge, each step closer to open water brings a change in footing. The mud has less root material in it and is less firmly bound together. It begins to ooze around your shoes. On the edges of the creeks, especially the larger ones, there may be natural levees where the ground is higher. Here the rising tide meets its first real resistance as it spills over the creek banks and has to flow between the close-set plants. Here it is slowed and drops the mud it may be carrying. Here too, especially after a series of tides, lower than usual, the ground is firm and even dry and hard.

Down toward the creek, where the mud is watered at each tide, the soil is as muddy as you can find anywhere. When you try to walk across to the water at low tide, across the exposed mud where the marsh grass does not grow, hip boots are not high enough to keep you from getting muddy. The boots are pulled off on the first or second step when they have sunk deep into the clutching zone. There are no roots to give solidarity, nothing but the mud and water fighting a shifting battle to hold the area.

At low tide the salt marsh is a vast field of grasses with slightly higher grasses sticking up along the creeks and uniformly tall grass elsewhere. The effect is like that of a great flat meadow. At high tide, the look is the same, a wide flat sea of grass but with a great deal of water showing. The marsh is still marsh, but spears of grass are sticking up through water, a world of water where land was before, each blade of grass a little island, each island a refuge for the marsh animals which do not like or cannot stand submersion in salt water.

This book is about the marshes of the East Coast of North America: how they were formed; why they continue to exist; the interplay of plants and animals; and the effect of that influential animal, man.

PART I

Birth and Death of a Marsh

1. Birth

ABOUT FIFTY THOUSAND YEARS AGO, A PRODIGIOUS ICE
sheet, the Laurentide Glacier, came down out of the
north and pressed across Canada and the northern part
of the United States. A vast complex of similar ice
sheets extended over other areas of the world. The
climate and sea level changed dramatically. Plants and
animals accommodated to the changes, moved south, or
died.

The glacier eventually reached a southern limit. The
melting of the edge was matched by the southern movement of the ice mass in response to the additional
weight of ice being continually added in the north.
Rocks, sands, and gravels scraped from the land by the
ice were piled up at this southern limit. The piles, called
moraines, grew as years passed. A continual flow of
meltwater ran out from the ice in streams. These were
milky from the rock flour they carried: rocks ground to
dust by the weight of the ice. Sands and gravels were
also washed out by the water and even rocks were
rolled along for a short distance where the flow was
swiftest. All this debris was spread out as outwash
plains in front of the moraines.

Then the ice retreated for a short distance and again
paused for hundreds or thousands of years. Another
moraine was laid down and more outwash plains deposited. These moraines and plains were small in relation to
the mass of ice responsible for them but look large in the

present landscape and are called Long Island, Martha's Vineyard, Nantucket, and Cape Cod.

Suddenly, for no certain reason, the climate changed. Ice was no longer added to the center of the glacier and it no longer moved south. The glacier began to melt. Thinner places disappeared first and the sheet broke up, first at the southern edge, then more generally. Finally the Laurentide Glacier disappeared altogether.

The landscape of the glacier was strange and awesome. Far from its edges, the five thousand to ten thousand feet thick ice sheet was probably quite flat and covered deeply with snow as the Greenland Glacier is now. A thin layer of soil accumulated on top of the edge of the ice sheet as the dust and debris, which had been locked in the ice, was freed by melting. This soil was augmented by dust blown onto the ice sheet from the surrounding, uncovered countryside. Small plants, larger plants, and even spruce forests grew atop the accumulated soil. Streams of cold ice melt ran in rivulets between the trees. Occasionally a huge crack would open up in the surface soil, exposing the mass of clear ice below.

This landscape was a temporary affair and changed as melting occurred. The forests eventually fell as the base beneath them melted and were swept away in the ice melt.

Water was everywhere. It ran in streams and rivers on rocky beds over the surface of the ice. It issued from the ice where it had run in tunnels cut in the glacier. It came forth in fountains and artesian springs that burst out of cracks in the ice. The springs were fed by a system of internal rivers which coursed through the ice from northern elevations. The water carried with it a mixture of rock flour and sand: a very erosive, fluid sandpaper that cut through ice and rock alike.

Before the new soil was finally held in place by a plant cover, it blew everywhere on the fierce winds that raced down from the snowy ice uplands. The scene was desolate but was one that was gradually to change. At times dust covered everything: ice, sand, till, and plants. Finally it was washed down into the mud and became part of the soil. It became a good soil on which wind-blown seeds soon sprouted.

Rain fell in torrents. Dense fogs wet the new plants. Their roots were watered by frigid water from the melting ice. Nutrient rich rock flours fertilized the new seedlings. The plants grew abundantly and where they flourished atop the glacier, they insulated the ice below.

Unusually well-protected areas of ice remained unmelted long after the main mass of ice had disappeared. The climate steadily grew warmer and eventually the sheltered ice, too, melted. When it did the forests atop the ice fell, leaving great holes in the landscape. If they were deep enough, the holes became lakes. If they were not, they became kettle holes, rounded depressions in the ground which grew new forests at the new lower level.

Torrents of meltwater from the complex of glaciers around the world ran into the sea. The level of the sea rose. While the land was being uncovered in the north by melting ice, it was being covered again in the south by rising sea. Land which had carried the crushing weight of the glacier sprang up when relieved of its burden and so the land rose as well as the sea.

These dramatic changes occurred at a rapid rate during the early waning of the ice. The edge of the sea was colonized by plants. Marsh plants grew, only to be drowned. More marshes started again, only to be destroyed. In this era of cataclysmic change, there was no time for extensive marsh development.

There came a time, however, when the ice remained only in the distant north. The land by now had finished its rapid rebound. The advance of the sea slowed. Plants, as well as changes in climate and sea level, began to work their slow effect on the features of the earth's surface where the land met the sea.

The retreat of the Laurentide Glacier occurred about ten thousand years ago. At this time, at a point along the New England coast, there was a flooded river valley which had carried glacial meltwater and rainwater to the sea. It was drowned at its mouth by the rise of the sea and shut off from its ancient sources of water by tons of glacial debris. A stream ran down to it from the surrounding hills. Well-worn, low mountains protruded from the flooded valley and protected the inner part of a small cove from waves and winds.

A flock of shorebirds settled on the protected shore in their northward search for tundra on which to nest. On the previous day, they had rested on wet mud on a salt marsh miles to the south. When they settled to rest the following day, the mud which had dried on their feet flaked off. In the mud were the seeds of marsh plants. Perhaps some seeds germinated and survived the first time they were deposited on the barren shore, or perhaps there were many arrivals and reseedings before the first plants took hold successfully, but successful they eventually were.

Grass began to grow at the edge of the water where the tides covered the ground less than half of the time. *Spartina alterniflora*, a tall coarse grass, grew above mid-tide level while *Spartina patens*, a finely textured relative, grew above the *S. alterniflora* at high water level. Other plants shared small areas of the tidal region. Sea lavender bloomed among the *Spartinas*. A stubby little plant with water-swollen stems, *Salicornia*, grew on sandy banks along the water's edge.

Salt marshes lay to the south and the east around the shores of a large island. For, where George's Bank now provides good fishing ground, it then provided a nesting area for wandering birds, grazing for mammoths and caribou, and coves where *Spartina* formed salt marshes. The marshes to the south grew and remained. Those to the east were eventually drowned and destroyed by the sea which had given them life.

The particular bit of marsh where the birds had rested continued to grow. Sand washed down the river from recently uncovered land and was carried into the sheltered cove. The sand was then moved along the shore by the winds, waves, and currents. Some of it was deposited in the cove and some built up a protective bar across the cove entrance. Small streams brought light soil material, fine particles of silt and clay, to the sea, some of which settled about the stems and roots of flourishing *Spartina*.

Gradually, as more and more sediment was trapped, and the plant roots bound it into a firm peat, the marsh grew in level and size. It reached out into the water over the sand which had been added to the cove. It reached high water level and above, at which time *Spartina alterniflora* gave ground to *Spartina patens*, with its greater ability to live in high marsh. The *S. patens* area enlarged as the marsh grew in total extent.

As new environments developed, animals moved into the marsh. Soft-shell clam and quahog larvae drifted in with the tide and settled in the soft mud around the pioneering stalks of marsh grass before the mud became filled with roots.

With the clams came clam-eating animals: families of raccoons and families of mink. Annelids and snails colonized the marsh also by means of their floating larvae. Insects flew in to lay eggs, and birds flew in to feed on the insects.

Sea level continued to rise. Plant growth raised the level of the marsh to keep step with the changing sea level. *Spartina patens* marsh flourished atop an accumulated layer of peat, formed from the roots and leaves of previous growth. Broken up, but not completely decomposed, the peat developed just fast enough to keep up with the water's rise and the sinking of the marsh surface as underlying peat was compressed by the weight of new forming peat.

As the sea level rose, the marsh extended inland over the edges of what had been land. Freshwater grasses and shrubs were engulfed by flooding salt water. Marsh grasses moved in. Land plant remains were buried under the marsh.

Lying just inland from the salt marsh, there was a shallow kettle hole made by glacial melting. Grass and trees grew on the bottom of the hole, which had been above the water table when it formed. As the water table rose with the rising sea level, a small pond formed with sedges and cattail around its edge. The kettle hole became filled with debris and peat from freshwater plants that had died under the advance of the marsh. Eventually a swamp developed around the pond. The bottom of the pond also filled but not enough to permit the growth of plants. It remained open water.

Gradually the kettle hole progressed to cedar swamp. Large trees grew over most of its area, but there remained a grassy zone in the center surrounding the pond.

The sea level rose to the point where the cedar swamp and the salt marsh met along the little stream that drained the kettle hole. Freshwater and a dam of cattail kept the seawater out. For a time, the swamp lived on, but its future was tenuous. The dense cedars shaded the ground beneath themselves so that the growth of the swamp slowed. But the sea level did not slow its rise. It continued to encroach on the land, adding a foot of height every hundred years.

One autumn there was an unusually severe storm. Seawater blew directly into the cove. The devastation of the storm was heightened by the effects of a very high tide. Even the heavy rains accompanying the storm were not enough to keep seawater out of the swamp. The soil became soaked with salt.

The following spring, none of the freshwater plants leafed out and the cedars were dead. With little to hold it back, the sea invaded the area regularly. *Spartina* enlarged its domain into the now salty soil and claimed the entire area of the old swamp.

Some of the dead cedars stood for years, serving as perches for osprey. Generations of the birds lived in nests of sticks in the top of a large old rotting tree until it blew down in a gale. The last visible evidence of the

Shorebirds feeding on the salt marsh:
short-billed dowitcher, solitary sandpiper, lesser yellowlegs

freshwater swamp became entirely buried in the salt marsh.

There remained, deep under the surface, a layer of dark peat composed of freshwater plants dotted with the stumps of the forest which once covered the region. The salt marsh peat layer on top became so deep that if the trees still stood, only the highest ones would be able to reach into the air through the thick blanket of *Spartina* remains. The last vestige of the kettle hole was the small pond in its center. It never filled but remained a "bottomless" hole in the marsh.

As the sea rose and the marsh rose with it, the cove gradually disappeared. Sand washed in by the tide was slowly colonized, first by *S. alterniflora* and then by *S. patens*.

Pools formed on the marsh where the grass was killed for a variety of reasons. The pools became individual, isolated worlds inhabited by insects and bacteria. Sheets of algae grew across the bottom. Fish swam into the pools during some high tides, were trapped, and lived for weeks or months before another high tide might liberate them.

Sometimes shallow pools were formed by extra high tides which drove water up to shallow depressions lying on the highest parts of the marsh next to the land. The pools might remain days or even weeks but life in the pools was less lasting. Water evaporated and salts were concentrated until they finally settled out on the bottom. As only a few bacteria are suited to live in strong brine, most of the residents died.

Ducks and shorebirds flying north and south during their migrations were attracted to all of the pools. Thousands of birds stopped to rest on their long flights. Yellowlegs stalked in the shallows and ducks upended in the pools to eat widgeon grass growing there. Dainty, graceful solitary sandpipers trembled their feet in the shallow pools without roiling the water, stirring up insects from the bottom. Dowitchers fed around the pool edges. Often they continued to jab their long bills in the mud well after dark, when other shorebirds had long since settled for the night. Some of the ducks, which stopped in the spring, stayed all summer to raise young. They grew and fattened themselves on the production of the marsh before undertaking the southward fall migration.

As the marsh grew, it and the bay became more productive. It became possible for larger numbers of fish to live in the water and larger numbers of animals to be supported on the surface soils. As the numbers of animals increased, so did the number of species.

A pair of bald eagles moved in to nest in the tallest pine on a high spot near the edge of the marsh. The birds ate fish picked up along the shore, fish stolen from the ospreys, which were smaller but better hunters, injured and sick ducks on the ponds, rabbits, mice, and other small animals on the marsh.

Marsh hawks, called harriers, nested on a hillock projecting out of the marsh and could be seen sailing above the grass searching for white-footed mice running between the *S. patens* stems, and for sharp-tailed sparrows, also running mouselike through the grass. Short-eared owls hawked over the marsh, competing with the harriers for the same food. The owls and harriers could not have been supported on the earlier marsh as it had been too small to support the large, inefficient hunters.

A pair of black-crowned night herons nested in a tree on an island in a freshwater pond near the marsh. At night they fished the marsh creeks. The parent birds raised a successful clutch. The following year the young birds returned with their mates, accompanied by other couples picked up in their migration. More birds were attracted the following year. In a short time there was a noisy, smelly hubbub on the island every summer. Hundreds of heron chicks were fed thousands of fish by their parents, and grew to adulthood.

The fish population was not depleted, nor were the mice and small birds fed upon by the raptors, for the predators snatched those individuals easiest to catch, the weak and lame. With these disposed of, the fish and game populations became healthier than ever.

Not all was idyllic about the growth of the marsh. Occasional but devastating disasters overtook both plants and animals. An unusually severe winter, with strong gales, sent great masses of ice and water over the end of the sandspit separating the ocean from the marsh. The surface of the soil was torn off. With the stabilizing plant cover gone, that part of the marsh eroded severely in the early spring storms. The slow advance of sediment deposit and plant growth repaired the damage in two hundred years.

Some floods were brought on by high wind-driven waves during seasonal hurricanes. Tons of rainwater were dumped on the marsh, compounding the wave damage. Thousands of birds, mammals and insects were drowned. The population of animals was small for a time, but reinstated itself, as the life-giving plants were not killed. New individuals of the depleted species moved into the marsh and the scanty survivors increased with the advent of amiable weather.

During occasional cold foggy summers the grass grew

Slumped bank of Spartina *at low tide*

poorly. Many animals perished from exposure. During hot dry seasons the marsh pools were desiccated or evaporated until the salt concentration killed the animals. Occasional fires started by lightning in nearby forests spread onto the surface of the marsh when the grass was dry in autumn. At such times many animals were killed, especially those which moved slowly and those which could not draw themselves down to safety under the blanket of wet, insulating mud.

In spite of these large and small disasters, the marsh continued to exist and grow. The rising sea permitted it to spread out over what had been land ten feet above sea level a thousand years before. The hillock which supported the eagles' pine became an island in the marsh but eventually disappeared entirely beneath the grass. Eagle descendants, many generations distant from the first pair, moved from tree to tree inland as their home trees died and blew down or were engulfed by marsh.

The marsh grew out into the water and filled the upper part of the bay. Channels in the bay were kept open by the tides, and these became the marsh creeks.

Because they were creeks of fast flowing water, their banks eroded along the outward edge of curves and dumped the eroded sediment on the inward edge of curves farther along. The outward banks became undercut and caved in. *Spartina* growth along the top of the bank slumped down in the mud. Some plants lived on but some died when they were carried too far into the intertidal region to survive. The inside of the curves became gently sloping mudbanks into which clams burrowed and on which *Spartina* propagated to the limit of its ability.

Changes in the creek meanders were especially heightened by any heavy rain which fell during low tide. During such rains, water accumulated on top the marsh and ran out over its edges down to the creeks. The water ran in channels, soaked into the mud and caused small mudslides along the creek banks where undercutting had taken the support from under the surface of the marsh.

The slides were quickly swept away by the currents in the large creeks. New sediment filled the scars. In smaller creeks where currents were never strong, the slumped blocks of mud remained standing, held together by *Spartina* roots. Sometimes several blocks of mud ridged with marsh grass slipped down until the creek was split into several streams. Eventually the islands were washed downcreek, worn away at the unprotected base until the top collapsed. Then the creeks resumed their look and followed their former course.

The meanderings of the creeks were not widespread, but as curves developed, they grew more and more pronounced until they were loops returning upon themselves. Then they would cut themselves off at the base and flow straight again. The abandoned loop would fill with sediment and would soon be reclaimed by *Spartina*.

The marsh had been born, had grown, and had been populated by plants and animals. Continual and gradual changes occurred but the salt marsh was firmly established.

A large part of the bay was never to be bay again.

2. Invasion

ONE DAY INTO THE MARSH CAME A MAN, AN INDIAN. He hunted by himself for a day and then brought other hunters the following day for the abundant game he had discovered in this virgin territory. There was no nearby village. Food had been short for the Indians that summer and hunters had ranged farther and farther from the home village. But that winter all that remained of the hunting expeditions were a few duck feathers and the black remains of a wood fire at the edge of the marsh.

Later, a hunting village was established only a short distance inland from the marsh in the bay. The early men, few in number, were content to live with nature. They took what was necessary for survival. There was more than enough production for all and the marsh was but little affected by the invasion of this new animal species. But it was visited more and more regularly. Trails were worn into the high parts of the marsh. At the end of the trails lay rich clam beds.

The Indians were little more important to the marsh than were the bears which came to fish the upper end of a freshwater creek nearby. Deer came onto the marsh to catch the breeze when flies swarmed in to the woods and browsed the vegetation along the landward marsh edge.

An occasional wolf prowled through the *Spartina* in his wide-ranging search for prey, looking especially for muskrats which lived in the fresher, cattail areas. Foxes looked for young ducklings in the creeks. Cougars, weasels, bobcats, skunks, raccoons, and mink wandered out onto the marsh, preyed and were preyed upon.

The Indians left in the winters but returned the following springs. They fished the creeks when the sun warmed the inland freshwaters before the sea lost its chill. Alewife, a herring, came up through the marsh in large numbers on their way to spawning grounds. The Indians made their way to the herring runs guided by clouds of gulls interspersed with ospreys and eagles, screaming and fighting over captured fish. The Indians bailed large numbers of alewife into woven twig baskets which they carried back to the village. They feasted on the fish. More were used to fertilize their corn to encourage a decent crop from the poor sandy soil.

Paths of trampled grass leading to the alewife creeks grew up again during the year after the herring had stopped running. New paths were worn through the grass the following year which were then obliterated by time and disuse.

In the shallow parts of the water in front of the marsh the Indians built fish traps constructed of long lines of brushwood stuck into the sand. When fish, swimming along the edge of the grass at high tide, met the barrier of brush, they turned into deeper water, moving along the brush row. At the end of the row they were caught in an enclosure in which they milled around until the tide fell. Then the Indians scooped them from the shallow water as they did the alewife.

The fish trap remained in the same general location for generations, several hundred years. Brush was replaced as it was washed away or broken. In time, when sediment filled the shallows which led into the trap, it was abandoned and marsh grass colonized the area. The brush remained in the sand for several years and helped to accelerate the marsh growth by slowing the passage of water so that sediment was deposited. The inner brush circle of the trap was finally buried and preserved for hundreds of years in the mud. This first important effect of man on the marsh was constructive.

As well as the alewife, the Indians took large numbers of shellfish from the pools in the growing parts of the marsh where *Spartina* roots had not yet changed the soft mud into firm ground. These collecting efforts destroyed bits of marsh grass and made slight erosion but the damage was quickly repaired by the robust *Spartina* plants.

The effects of the several thousand year tenure of the Indians were exceedingly slight. There were not many Indians and there was a lot of marsh. At the height of the Indian population there were still only a few hundred individuals living in the village. To us the environs would have seemed completely wild. Yet it was not altogether wild.

A bit of civilization crept in when the Indians cleared land for crops and instituted a system of crop rotation allowing the fields to lie fallow alternate years. Corn, squash, and beans were fertilized with fish and seaweed gathered from the marsh. There was little erosion from the cultivated land. Because of the crop fertilization and rotation, it was possible to harvest the same fields for generations. The Indians did not exhaust the fields as did the Englishmen who later grew tobacco in the central Atlantic colonies.

When winter came the Indians moved from their summer residence near the marsh to permanent winter villages up in the river valleys. The seasonal migrations were quite like they are today, except for the time necessary to cover the ground between the two villages. Some families stayed late in the fall, for the lingering warmth of the sea kept their gardens green longer than the vegetation in the river valleys. There was also the fall hunting of marsh birds.

Hunting began when the earliest shorebirds came through in July on their way south after a quick nesting trip in the north. Flocks of trusting dowitchers probed the mud vertically with their long bills. Pectoral sandpipers stalked crickets in the *S. patens* marshes. Other shorebirds followed. The greatest flocks and best hunting came late in summer when the migrations were in full swing. The migrant birds settled on the marsh to feed and rest. When the shorebirds flew 'on, they were replaced by rafts of ducks and gaggles of geese.

It was on the marsh creeks that the first Europeans to invade the area met the Indians. The Europeans were fishermen who came to the New World to seek the wonderful fishing grounds that had been reported. They found the shelter of the bay by the marsh and anchored there to mend their boats and fishing gear. A party of sailors went up in the marsh creeks to look for freshwater and meat. They came face to face with the Indians who were coming down the marsh creeks to look at them. After a few uneasy moments on each side, each decided the other was friendly. The Indians had meat and vegetables. The Europeans had knives and fishhooks. Negotiations for an exchange began at once.

Later fur traders came. When they could, they traded beads and worthless trinkets. The wiser Indians demanded iron tools for their valuable furs. The fishermen continued to come at irregular intervals. These hardy sailors, dark-complexioned men from Spain and Portugal, sailed their small ships across the Atlantic Ocean for fish. They visited the bay and marsh only when beset by troubles.

About a hundred years after Europeans had been coming regularly to trade with the Indians, and shortly before the first colonists were to arrive, serious trouble arose. The Indians and the English, who were by then doing most of the trading along the coast wherein the marsh was located, were in dispute. Differences intensified and boiled up into war. Perhaps the Indians ran out of furs or the English out of trade goods. Perhaps there was deception on both sides. But the merits of the two sides as fighting teams were never really tested. Between the time of the beginning of hostilities and the coming of the first colonists, a disease, probably one of the communicable diseases of childhood to which Englishmen were immune, killed a large number of the Indians. They thought the disaster to be the result of a curse put upon them by the foreigners. The few Indians left alive fled from the coastal villages. For a time men, both Indian and European, disappeared from the marsh.

As soon as the first settlers came from Europe, the uncorrupted epoch of the marsh ended. From that time on a major force shaping the life of the salt marsh was the activities of men.

The shores of the bay marsh were occupied very early in the settlement of New England. To men coming from a well-gardened country with neat, one-crop fields, the salt marsh presented a favorable sight in the untamed landscape. Here was cleared pasture. Here was a hay field waiting to be cut.

Among the earliest arrivals on the shore near the marsh were a hard-working, wiry Englishman, John Deacon, and his wife Abigail. The Deacons chose a likely spot for their homesite on a creek with depth enough to float a small boat. They had easy access from the water on one side but only rough land access from the other.

Since it was the main and most landward creek in the marsh, it carried freshwater from land runoff as well as tidal water. Except for the muddy banks of the main creek and its equally muddy but smaller tributaries, the marsh had developed into high marsh, drier than wet. John Deacon decided early that this excellent pasture should be used. He had been a smith in England and had brought tongs and hammers. He traded his skill for a cow with calf. The cow was a tired skinny animal just arrived from England, but she and the heifer she dropped grew sleek on the marsh grass. John simply let them wander at will where there was available food.

The Deacons were too busy building, clearing and trying to get gardens started in those first years to fence in the growing cattle herd, soon five head, as they had lost no time breeding the calf when she reached the age. There was little need to build fences. The animals moved from pasture to greener pasture. In those years the greener pastures were the marshes. The cattle spent considerable time in the woods browsing, but for hearty grazing they always moved back to the salt hay flats. It was soon apparent that the unrestrained cattle damaged the surface soils of the marsh but not dangerously so.

One day the old cow slipped on the soft sides of a tidal pool. She tried to regain her footing but slipped farther and farther into the soft ooze. John Deacon, unable to move her, was finally forced to shoot her. There were a few dark days in the Deacon household. The old cow had been their first and she was still good for a few more calves. Even worse, John had been forced to waste ball and powder with nothing to show for it on the table.

Other farmers were having the same difficulty. Cattle had to be kept off the dangerous marsh but there were no fenced pastures in which to confine them. Fences were time-consuming to build. Time spent building fences was less time spent doing the multitude of jobs necessary to keep a family alive in the harsh new world. So fences were built only around gardens, to keep cattle out, not to fence them in.

By now twenty farms were strewn along the rise bordering the marsh. The boys took turns acting as common drovers to keep cattle off the marsh and to bring them back to owners for milking in the evening.

With the cattle off the marsh, the grass grew undisturbed again. More hay could be cut for the winter and more was needed as the numbers of farms and cows increased.

John Deacon and two other men, close neighbors who would call on him for a similar service, took scythes out to mow the marsh in August when the grass was tall but not yet mature. At this season it made the best fodder, as the men knew from their experiences with upland grasses. They chose neap tides for their work when the salt hay marsh was not flooded. The men moved along, three abreast, and cut the high marsh grasses. After the hay was cured the men gathered it by pitchfork and piled it into stacks. They also cut what they could of the tall *S. alterniflora*, thatch as it was called. Some areas along the banks of the creeks were difficult to cut but on the flat new growths of marsh it was easier.

On the lower reaches sure to be flooded, the salt hay was cut and carried to the upland, perhaps to be put in the barn. On the high marsh, the hay was piled on small poles driven into the surface of the soil in clusters about two feet high and two feet apart. On these groups of small pilings, called staddles, the hay was safe from high tides. The hay was collected in the fall if necessary, but usually it was left until winter came and the frozen marsh surface could support an ox team and sledge.

Haying on the marsh

Sometimes an unusually high tide occurred when a regular high was made higher by strong winds in an autumn storm. Then the carefully piled haystacks floated off the staddles intact and finally lodged up against the land somewhere. The farmers went out, tried to locate and identify their own. One, less generous than his neighbors, put a marked stick into his stacks for identification and was accused of putting similar sticks into any lost stack he came across.

The house John and his neighbors built contained three rooms at first, snug and tight. Its heavy wood frame was surfaced with clapboards. The roof of thatch was put on in the old style carried over from English thatchers but the thatch came not from an upland cornfield as it had in England, but from the rugged *S. alterniflora* especially selected from the lush growth along the tidal creeks.

The thatched roof caught fire on two occasions from flying chimney sparks. Both times John and Abigail were lucky enough to discover the fire in time to climb to the roof and pitch the burning thatch to the ground.

In time there were quite a number of Deacon children surrounding the hearth and small hands helped with the farm and marsh chores. John Deacon had borrowed a little lore from the Indians. Fishing and shellfishing did not stop because one group of men supplanted another. The food gathering continued but the methods changed. Men still waited for the warming in spring to herald the coming of the alewife, now also called sawbelly. They went down, entire families together with nets, to catch the fish. They dammed the creeks and waited for the dammed area to fill with fish. Then they harvested. Like the Indians, the colonists carried the fish back to the fields where they planted them along with the corn for fertilizer.

Alewife season was one of feast. Some of the fish were eaten fresh or pickled and some salted for future use. The herring were a welcomed item in a diet which was beginning to bore after the long winter of living on stored foods from last year's harvest.

John and the children watched bald eagles with fully developed white heads, soaring over the creeks to get their share of the alewife bounty. They watched flocks of gulls pick up the silvery fish from the water and carry them to nearby dry spots where they slit the belly of the fish open with their beaks and extracted roe. The Deacons took a lesson from the birds and gathered only roe to fry for a meal when they had already preserved as many fish as they needed.

The marsh continued to grow and now it extended for miles up and down the bay from its original beginnings. More land was cleared and more farms built along those miles. Roads were cut through the wilderness but they remained rough and often rutted. Travel was still difficult inland.

Farmers, seeking the easiest means of transport, turned to boating through the marsh creeks on their way to market at the village which was growing midway along the marsh. The village was only a small cluster of houses early in its existence, but it boasted a town landing consisting of a crude ramp of stones and logs. A roadway was built across the high marsh to the landing. Eventually the creek was dug out and enlarged and a small pier built.

Soon coastal schooners sailed up the creek at high tide. The schooners, if they were caught between tides, waited out the hours with their bottoms in the mud. If it took a certain amount of time to get the schooner up the twisting creek, it was of small concern to the townsmen. However, it was of concern to the schooner's crew and the new merchant class developing in the village. The pier was often crowded with loads of lumber and foundation stones from northern New England. Some schooners brought cargo from old England too, dishes, furniture, and tools. When empty, the boats were loaded with farm and fishing produce. The lumber and stones were used to build more houses in the village, which grew vigorously.

3. Civilization

TRADE BECAME IMPORTANT. ROADS WERE STILL BAD, with many of them being no more than old Indian trails. The village eventually became large enough so that some form of government became necessary. The town meeting, during which men could voice their opinions from the floor on all town business, became a yearly event. After a heated discussion one year, it was voted by a bare majority to improve access to the sea. The proposal was to cut off two bends of the tidal creek with channels so that boat passage up the creek would be more quickly made. Progress was on the move with the growing population.

There was considerable objection from the farmers who didn't look forward to getting into the mud to accomplish the part of the digging they knew would be their lot. The sailors, they said, had plenty of time for the trip. The farmers lost and the ditches were dug. Tidewater was forced into a new path, shorter and more direct through the marsh. But the village fathers had only caused the creek to follow a course it had pursued several centuries before and could, if left to nature, pursue again.

Clams settled in the mud of the new cut. *Spartina* ventured out into the water as far as it could grow. Clams also were plentiful in the marsh pools where they grew to fine size. Clamming was not yet an industry. As there was little market, no men dug them as an occupation. The digging fell to the boys and sometimes girls, who kept individual families supplied.

The children walked over the marsh at low tide to the pools, waded into the water barefoot and felt for the hard, round bivalves with their toes. More often than not they filled their baskets.

It was the children who best knew the call of the strange marsh heron, the bittern. On warm spring evenings they heard the thump-thump of the bittern's love song and called him the thunder-pumper or stake driver. They stole quietly up to watch the bird gulp air, inflate his neck sack, and give out his little thumping thunder. They knew that the male beautified himself by exposing the long white feathers, normally hidden beneath his wings. When wooing, he erected the feathers and spread them behind the bent forward head and neck so that they looked like two small angel wings.

The children searched for the bittern's nest. If they were lucky or diligent, they might come upon a family of young bitterns hiding in the grass, pretending to be sticks, their bills pointing toward the sky. The only motion the baby birds would make would be an almost imperceptible movement of their feet as they edged away from danger. If a breeze caused the grass to bend and sway, the bitterns swayed also, maintaining the fiction that they were not really there at all.

From firsthand experience, the children knew what "thin as a rail" meant, from trying to trace the paths of elusive clapper rails as they threaded their way through the thick grass with rarely a disturbance of the leaves to give their presence away. They knew that the little black balls of down were tiny rail chicks following their parents through the grass. The parents stalked feeding fiddler crabs. When they caught a male crab, the birds would shake him until the large claw and body separated. Then it was an easy task to eat the defenseless crab.

If they were lucky, the children might find a nest

before the full clutch of eight to twelve clapper rail eggs was laid. The eggs would still be fresh for they knew the mother didn't warm them until the clutch was filled. The children searched out the inverted cone nests which were constructed of dead *Spartina* leaves poked into the mud anchored in place by living *Spartina* leaves. A find of edible eggs was rare, as the clapper rail never did heavily populate the northern marsh.

One year during the September storm season, a small coastal schooner on its way to the village landing was caught by a sudden squall and blown onto the marsh. It was an old boat and split along the keel. The crew abandoned ship and waded over the marsh to the Deacons' house. They were given a hot stew and blankets and directed out to a small barn. There they fared very well, sleeping on pallets of salt hay newly gathered. When the storm abated, they stripped what they could from the small boat and left her to the elements. Thereafter the children played in the rotting carcass. With time, all that remained of the boat were the ballast stones, resting as they were originally placed in her bilge, buried deep in the peat. Long before the boat finally rotted, John Deacon died. Abigail soon followed. But behind them they left children and grandchildren, a large farm of cleared meadow and cropland and a large tract of salt hay marsh.

The marsh grew faster than ever. The rise in sea level was slower than it had been in the earlier part of the marsh's history, but the sediment delivered to the sea and distributed by the waters was now greater than it had been at any time since the retreat of the ice.

Much of the land near the coast and almost all of the land near the marsh was cleared. The Deacons had plowed and cultivated for three generations with no thought of soil preservation.

Heavy rainfalls moved soil and sand off the low surrounding hills into the streams coursing into the marsh creeks and finally to the sea. The sand contributed to the protecting bars and enclosed more area into which the salt marsh could grow. It also built up the bottom of the bay. *Spartina alterniflora* extended claim to the new shallows and trapped soil there.

As the sandbars grew, the sand was often blown across the surface of the marsh during fierce winter gales. A layer of sand was deposited by winter, then covered by a layer of mud during the summer. The marsh preserved a record of alternating good and hard times like a tree does in its rings.

The growth of the marsh affected the existing high marsh areas very little. They could not grow faster than the sea level rose. *Spartina alterniflora* colonized large new tracts, many of which were quickly transformed into new high marsh. There was more salt hay for the cutting and frequent disputes arose over property lines. A changing salt marsh was hard to apportion.

The earliest colonists, like the Indians before them, were plagued by swarms of mosquitoes, biting midges, and attacking greenheads. The biting midges lived in the damp sand near land. Adults emerged fairly early in the spring ahead of other biting insects and served to remind the colonists that they were tied to the land. They could not get out of reach of the "no-see-ums," as they were named by the Indians.

The mosquitoes were a far greater problem, especially after a heavy rain. Minnows, which consume large numbers of larvae, could often neither reach nor survive in the pools on the high marsh, so there was always a plentiful supply of the noxious pests. A few families of black ducks cleaned out the pools in which they dabbled, but the mosquitoes were too many and the ducks too few. The insects went swiftly through their larval stage, pupated, and emerged ready for the blood meal that would insure eggs for the next generation.

House windows were unscreened and sanitation was primitive. Fevers accompanied the swarming of insects. The marsh became dangerous at these times. Children deserted their clam digging. Men would venture out onto the marsh only when a stiff wind was blowing. Women neglected their household duties and made cold suppers in the midst of fanning mosquitoes from the smallest children. The families were under siege with little help but a hand and a flyswatter.

When the spring attack of the mosquitoes was over, it was likely to be followed by an attack of fierce biting greenheads. In fall, the mosquitoes returned to attack once again. Dragonflies reduced the mosquito plague to some degree by gathering the pests in their basket legs and then eating them. Swallows fed on both the mosquitoes and greenheads. The birds dipped and swooped

Broken bay ice on marsh

over the marsh, filling their gullets. Young birds on the nest collected most of the bounty from their parents' throats. There was also some relief gained from burning the marsh in the autumn after the hay had been gathered. Greenhead eggs laid on the surface of the marsh were often destroyed in the burnings, but some eggs hatched before the burnings and some areas of marsh escaped the burnings altogether.

The greenheads seemed to be at their most obnoxious height during dry seasons. They were never as plentiful as the mosquitoes but their bite was much more painful. They tore through the skin of their victims with enough force to make blood flow. The greenheads were even more devastating to the animals, which had less ability than men to protect themselves. Horses and cows were sometimes made frantic in their effort to escape the biting insects. On a quiet day, no horse could be ridden near the marsh, for the mere sight and sound of the hungry flies on a heavily populated marsh made the mount uncontrollable.

The Deacons had wisely chosen to build their house on a little knoll that was open to the breeze from all sides. The fiercest manbiters stayed in the marsh. A few hundred yards inland was enough to leave most of the flies behind. The cattle did not fare as well, for the cattle-biting flies willingly followed their prey to the barns.

One day a new plant appeared in the marsh, a mallow. The children first found it blooming around the hull of the rotting schooner. Seeds had fallen from packing material and a few had taken root. Little attention was paid to the marshmallow at first until it spread up and down the coast. The colonists began recognizing it as the same marshmallow they had gathered in England to boil for a mucilaginous substance they had used as a cure for coughs and dysentery. If there was a little of the boiled substance left, the children were sure to be pleased with a batch of marshmallow confection.

The colonists turned more and more to the marsh to

set their table. Other than the marshmallow, they gathered marsh samphire for salads and pickles. The children were sent to gather the stubby, swollen little plants which gave a salty tanginess to salads. Eventually, with more store-bought food available, the samphire lost its flavor to the public. The garden-grown cucumber took over as the pickling favorite.

Men gathered meat from the marsh. Ducks and shorebirds were plentiful. In spring and fall they came to feed in the ponds and grass of the flats. Ducks ate snails, widgeon grass, small fish and shellfish. Shorebirds ate insects living on marsh grass, worms, snails, crabs, and occasionally, as in the case of the greater yellowlegs, small fish. Because the greater yellowlegs fed on fish, its flesh was not as tasty as the flesh of other birds, and it was shot only if hunting had been bad. Also, it was a wary bird and many a good shot was spoiled when the telltale, as it was called, sprang into the air with loud cries of alarm.

The guns of the early hunters were not good at a distance. The charge was as apt to go one way as another. But the hunting of shorebirds was aided by the birds' habits. They flew in tight flocks, twisting and turning as a unit. One shot into the flock would bring down many birds. Again, the telltale had an advantage. It didn't flock as did even its closest relative, the little telltale or lesser yellowlegs, but preferred to fly individually.

The doughbird or eskimo curlew and the simpleton or dunlin flew in tight bunches, broke and dodged when they were shot at, but then reformed and recircled, giving another good chance for a shot. The simpleton got its name from this pattern of flying. The doughbird was especially sought and many were killed to be salted away for the lean winter months.

Great flocks of doughbirds and golden plovers flew in constantly changing wedge shapes as they swept low over the new-mown high marsh looking for a spot that suited them. They would then settle, holding their wings high over their heads for a moment before carefully folding them and setting about feeding on grasshoppers and crickets. The birds were not at all shy and could be easily approached. Sometimes they didn't even fly away after shots had been discharged into the flock killing several birds. The colonists ate great-blackbacked gulls, herring gulls, and herons when times were lean, but the tasty meadowlark, called marsh quail, puddle ducks, and shorebirds were preferred.

Four generations of the Deacon family had been born in the house by the marsh. They continued in the old practices of farming, hunting, and hay gathering. Some of the overflow of children moved away to the gradually opening west: western Massachusetts, western Pennsylvania, and western New York.

A hundred and fifty years after the first thatch-covered cottage had been built by the Deacons, a long war came to the colonies. In the end, George the Third of England was the loser, and now the farm and marsh became free land instead of part of a colony attached to a mother country. The marsh was little affected by the turn of the political tide, but the lunar tides crept up a bit higher. More marsh was regularly flooded and more hay marsh developed.

A bird commonly associated with the south, the willet or humility, tried to colonize the marsh but the increase of the human population doomed the colony. It was shot out before it became firmly established.

Subtle changes occurred to the countryside. Woodlands were almost completely cleared to pasture and cropland. The population of white-tailed deer decreased dramatically with their woodland cover gone. A few strayed onto the marsh but did not stay since there was little cover there, too. Raccoons decreased for the same reason. The number of individual animals which lived on the marsh lessened because more area was cut for hay needed to feed the increased numbers of domestic cattle on the pastures.

Not all animals declined. Upland plovers increased

on the pastures and field edges next to the marshes and could often be found feeding on the high marsh. Meadowlarks in large numbers sang from fence posts and hay staddles.

The growing human population, with indifference to sanitation, supported large numbers of a new animal that made its way into the country. It was in no means restricted to the town where the population was concentrated, but made its way over the countryside and into the marsh. Where white-footed mice had always lived on the landward edge of the marsh, they were joined by the Norway or brown rat, *Rattus norvegicus*. According to the British, the rat made its way over with the colonists. According to the colonists, the rat made its way over with the British. But the rat, ignorant of the politics of the situation, made its way over with whom it could. At first it lived where it disembarked, near the docks. But then it quickly availed itself of the excellent coastwise transport and rode the schooners north and south.

The rat reached every village and farm near the coast and then spread by other transport into the hinterland. It found good pickings along the coast where food was cast up by the sea. But the rat's tastes were unlimited. If little in the way of dead sea life was to be found, it turned its attention to stored animal food. It attacked crops maturing in the fields. It turned to areas, most often marshes, where the increased population in villages and towns dumped debris and refuse. From that time on rats were always associated with dumps. The farmers cursed the rat then as often as farmers do now. *Rattus norvegicus* became a permanent unwanted guest.

With the removal of the forests and the turn to agriculture, the large birds of prey declined. Fewer eagles were seen scouting for dead or weak ducks. Fewer osprey quarreled with the eagles over a catch. The last tree housing an eagle nest near the Deacon farm blew down during a fierce northeastern gale one winter. The eagles circled the area the following spring, but as they couldn't find their tree, they abandoned the area altogether to settle in a pine tree at the edge of a lake some miles inland.

More and more land was put into agriculture but the pasturage couldn't keep up with the increase of farm animals. More and more hay was cut from the marsh.

The often harvested areas of marsh began showing the cumulative effects of hay cutting. The annual layer of dead grass which had previously been added to the top of the soil year after year was no longer formed. The soil surface was not protected by a natural mulch. Small animals which had lived in this cool, damp environment became less abundant, and the number of animals which had previously fed on them decreased. The grasses thinned at the upper edge of the zone where the balance between land and salt marsh was most precarious. The destruction of the natural mulch left the soil bare between the bunch grasses growing there. The bare soil became subject to increased erosion. During occasional heavy rains, much soil was carried away. Not often very far. It settled on the nearby marsh. The result was a flattening of the edge of the marsh and an increase in its lateral extent at a greater rate than was accounted for by the rise in sea level.

This erosion was unnoticed for many years. For the two hundred years the land had been settled, the marsh looked quite the same. Then, suddenly, due to unusually severe weather conditions, it changed dramatically.

One fall day, the morning was attended by strong winds and heavy rains. Water began accumulating on the ground, even on the porous sandy soil. The rainfall increased as the day continued, while the winds grew to full hurricane strength. Water runoff from the land into the marsh was extraordinarily heavy. Mud coursed and covered much of the surface of the landward part of the high marsh. Then the rain stopped and the eye of the storm passed. The wind shifted abruptly. It began to blow directly up the harbor, pushing a great amount of water before it into the marsh.

The water continued to rise and stayed high throughout the succeeding low tide period. The wind kept the tide piled high over the land so that it did not recede. When the tide finally fell, the ground for twenty feet inland from the former high tide mark was saturated with salt. The plants living in the twenty foot zone were dead.

The extent of the damage was not immediately apparent after the storm. Many plants near the sea had been badly burned by the salt but would survive as they had before. The clumps of grass that had been completely washed out were flushed away by the tides. But the ones that remained with a roothold had a chance to recover. The general leaf fall and browning of the grasses camouflaged the dead plants. Winter came before much recovery could occur, but the damage was obvious the following spring.

The Deacons had lost a large portion of upland meadow and gained an equal amount of marsh. The first plants to invade the new marsh soil were annual *Salicornias,* which were useless for hay. They were soon replaced by the high marsh grasses. Hay harvesting began again. But what had been "English hay" on the upland, was now "hay," a native American product.

4. Death

TRADE WAS INCREASING WITHIN THE NEW COUNTRY. Farms were no longer purely subsistence affairs. More traders visited the farms around the marsh and the farmers, consequently, needed more money. To get a little cash, the men hunted shorebirds for market.

Up until this period, the hunting of shorebirds had been a regular thing, done yearly, but only by the local people for their own use. Now there was a market in the cities, and ships traveling the coast were willing to add barrels of birds to their cargo. If many of the birds spoiled on the way and were thrown overboard on arrival in port, it was a small matter. There were plenty more. The supply seemed inexhaustible.

The birds were harvested like a crop with no element of sportsmanship. Some were shot, but ammunition cost money. A new method of hunting came into prominence. At night, when the birds were resting on the marsh, one hunter would crawl over the high marsh stubble with an unhooded lantern in his hands. Another hunter carrying a sack followed closely behind the first and simply reached around the lantern from the gloom and grabbed the dazzled, unprotesting birds. Each bird was quickly killed with the snap of its neck and tossed into the sack. A night's hunt saw sacks full of plover, robin snipe, and doughbirds.

Night hunting became so widespread that people finally became alarmed at the very definite possibility of destroying the flocks altogether. Laws were passed making the collecting of birds with lights illegal. Though many of the marsh owners scoffed at the possibility of decreasing such a large resource, in general they obeyed the laws and night gathering of shorebirds stopped. Hay remained the most important product of the marsh.

New methods of hay cutting were developed as the age of machinery moved in. Mowing by hand was supplanted by horse team and mowing machine. The marsh soils were not firm like the upland soils, so modifications were necessary. The mower was equipped with special wide wheels to distribute its weight over as much area as possible. That was the easy part of the modification. The horses had enough trouble just walking over the marsh unencumbered, but when they were attached to the mowers and leaned into their collars to pull the machine, their great hooves dug grooves into the soil, while the machine didn't move. Many a team got bogged down and had to be extracted from soft spots by other teams.

Special board wooden shoes were developed and fitted over the horse's hooves to provide extra surface over which to spread the load, as with the broad wheels of the mower. The horses did not like the large shoes and had to be fitted and trained in the barnyard before they could be trusted to the marsh. Drainage ditches were dug to make the marsh more firm and do away with low, wet spots. Some ditches were made with spades, but special two-bladed saws were also used to cut narrow channels in the high marsh peat.

Aside from the use of mechanical mowers, the haying went as usual. The cut hay was piled into small cocks, which were carried on long poles as a sedan chair is carried, and piled on the staddles. The hay cut near the creeks was gathered and piled on a double-hulled boat covered with a large deck which was then paddled along the creeks to a convenient landing from which the hay was stacked near a barn.

The hay on the accessible parts of the marsh was left stacked on the staddles. It was carefully piled up so that the outer layers acted like a thatched roof for the inner mass, keeping it dry during the autumn rains. When winter was well in possession of the marsh and the surface was frozen hard, the teams could be safely driven out to collect the hay. It was piled on wagons and taken directly to the barns as it had been two hundred years before.

The number of farms surrounding the Deacon homestead had gradually increased with the general increase in population. Then a great change came to the countryside. The railroad opened up the West. Farmers, tired of the rocky Eastern soil, moved out to the Midwestern states. At first the transplanted farmers used the agricultural methods they had used in the East. But farming in the new West was easier. The soil was fertile loam instead of rocks and sand. Once the land was cleared, it was easy to plow, especially using the newly developed steel moldboard plow.

News of the easy life out West spread. The exodus of farmers from New England was intensified. Then came the Civil War. The young men went to fight. Many developed a taste for travel and never came back to the farms on the marshes. It took two hundred years to build the homesteads and only ten years to depopulate them by half. In twenty years, three quarters of the farms were vacant. Barns and houses began to decay. Fields began to go back to forest.

Although many people left their farms, the land did not pass out of their possession. They continued to pay the small amount of taxes necessary to keep title. The Deacons were one of the few families that did not move off the land. Some of the Deacon offspring left for the riches of the far West and the Midwest, but there was always someone left on the homestead. Times were lean, however, and brought on an era of even greater plunder of the shorebirds than there had been two generations before. Since the night hunting laws had been passed, the bird population had increased somewhat.

Even though the bird population had not increased

dramatically, the human population along the East Coast had. Railroads ran supplies to city markets even more quickly than the boats had, so cities could be bigger. Emigration from Europe was reaching a high. The plunder of the shorebirds began in earnest.

The carnage of the sicklebill and long-billed curlew was especially intense, because, if one of their number fell, others of this shy bird fluttered over the dead or wounded. As more birds became easy marks and were shot, more individuals fluttered over the dead until often the entire flock would be shot.

In the same manner, smokelike clouds of doughbirds were killed. This tame, trusting species was easily decoyed or whistled up and settled on the marsh chattering more like blackbirds than the curlews they were.

The grass-bird or creaker and pectoral sandpiper came in small flocks to the harvested hay marshes. After alighting, the flock would split up to feed in shallow pools of water. They were not easily shot as they refused to come to decoys and crouched in the grass when approached. They would remain motionless until nearly stepped on, before springing suddenly into the air and flying erratically away.

Large marlin, now called marbled godwits, occasionally came in large flocks and were shot. Teeters, or spotted sandpipers, were left alone. These birds were quite solitary in habit, and so not worth the powder to shoot, especially when ten birds of another species might be brought down with one shot. Mud peeps or least sandpipers were not hunted for they were too small to be worth the effort.

The demand for birds increased so rapidly that other than local hunters began moving into the marshes. The professional hunters had, with the help of the farmers, exterminated the passenger pigeon. Farmers cut the forests in which they nested and hunters slaughtered them by the thousands for market. Now with the pigeon gone, the market-hunters turned their attention to the vast numbers of shorebirds.

In spring, much of their hunting was centered on the prairies of the Midwest. Here the golden plover, eskimo curlew, upland plover, and marbled godwit, on their way to the nesting grounds, were greedily killed. The effects of the Midwestern shoots were rapidly felt on the salt marshes. These species, which had previously visited the salt marsh on their way south, rapidly declined and disappeared from the fall migration. Hunting pressure was then directed to the smaller and less desirable species. At the same time, there were groups of "sportsmen" who came from the cities to hunt.

The Deacons supplied a sports club with blinds, boats and decoys for hunting on the marsh. The club members came in spring and fall. Professional hunters were not allowed on the Deacon marsh but there was some illegal shooting there as well as on all other marshes in the area.

During the best hunting years, the supply of birds was plentiful. Even on the worst days, blinds in the *Spartina* were always good for a number of birds, especially at low water, when the birds flying past would settle among the decoys placed in the water near a sandspit. If no flock ventured by, they would be whistled up. Sportsmen, to whom good hunting meant a large bag, could count on taking hundreds of birds of all sizes on a good day.

To other men, shooting was more sport when the birds had a better chance to escape. They hunted by stalking birds across the marsh. Many of the shorebirds were so trusting that even after they had been shot almost to extinction, it made small difference in what manner they were hunted. Others were wary and offered better sport. The telltales or yellowlegs were notorious for taking alarm and calling to all other birds within hearing. The jack or hudsonian curlew was too wary to be pursued for anything but sport. The blackbreast, black-bellied plover, was alert and suspicious, unlike its golden relative. A bag of blackbreast was considered a tribute to a hunter's skill at a time when an equal number of golden plover merely meant that a man could point a gun and fire.

The professional and sports hunting took such a terrible toll of birds that many species were in real danger of extinction. Men shot peeps, the smallest shorebirds no larger than sparrows, because the population of larger birds was so drastically reduced. There finally came the time when a day's hunt might scare up only a bird or two. Even the notoriously tame solitary sandpiper would jump up and fly away at the first approach of man.

Hunting was finally outlawed except in spring and fall and finally shorebird hunting was completely stopped by federal law. Duck hunting was still allowed, but only in the fall season.

The duck population then began to increase. The marsh pools filled with puddle-dabbling ducks upending for food on the bottom. Black ducks ate snails and widgeons ate widgeon grass. Blue-wing teal arrived early in the season and dabbled for mosquito larvae and other insects while shovelers used their wide bills to strain tiny crustaceans and debris from the ooze on the bottom of the pools. They sat in small groups on the pools up in the marsh and rested on the creeks and in the water of the harbor when not feeding.

The First World War came. The Deacon boys of draft age were taken into the army. The family moved to the city. Hay on the marsh was left uncut and the house began to fall in disrepair.

Forest reclaimed most of the farmland around the marsh. What had been village at the head of navigation on the Deacons' creek was now represented by only three houses back from the marsh and a number of cellar holes and chimney foundations.

Deacon children still played on the marsh and in its creeks as their ancestors had, but they lived in the old house only in the summer. Like all children they explored when given the chance. They poled around in the creeks in a small boat and played at pirates. In the spring, they saw whistlers or golden-eyes displaying. The drake put his head forward, then suddenly stretched upward, gave a harsh call and snapped his head back until it touched his rump. The female lay with her head forward on the water as if she were dead. But it was only a hoax. Later she would fly up, very much alive.

The children also saw the exuberant courtship flights of the male marsh hawk, bouncing up and down in the sky, as if he were a Yo-Yo on the end of a rubber tether attached to the clouds.

One fall they saw the last bald eagle ever to visit the marsh. It flapped off after being shot at, as it was stooping toward an injured duck.

During the boom of the 1920's, much of the Deacon farmland was sold to individuals who turned the area into a summer colony. The ancestral home and accompanying marshlands were not sold. In fact, they were not wanted by anyone. The great economic boom was followed by the bust of the 30's. The Deacon house was all but abandoned. The buildings deteriorated even further.

The marsh was gradually becoming polluted from wastes from the nearby summer colony. During the 1930's, a mosquito control commission was formed in the area, partly to control mosquitoes and partly to give work to men who could not find jobs. Ditches were dug to drain the pools in an effort to do away with breeding sites. Since the men were paid by the foot and it was easiest to dig near land, most of the ditching was accomplished close to land. Only occasionally were the ditches, by means of deeper ditches, connected to the creeks.

Even though the ditching was not well planned, it did drain many of the pools. But it had little effect on the mosquito population. The marsh pools, in which they had bred, had been drained long before by the farmers living around the marsh. Some of the old ditches had been clogged. Opening them was the easiest digging of all and the first action of the new ditchers. Subsequent ditching did more harm than good. It drained the small pools that attracted the ducks. The results were a few less mosquitoes and many less ducks.

The marsh became a nearly wild place again, a bit of unused area at the edge of a great city. The water was no longer pure but often had an oily film on its surface. The collection of debris along the high-water mark was composed of paper, cans, garbage, and wooden crates.

The 1930's ran into the 40's and brought the Second World War. The marsh was but little affected. Perhaps there was less collection of debris along the tide line because travel to the summer colony was restricted by gasoline rationing. The greatest changes to the marsh occurred at the end of the war. People had money to spend again, more freedom, and more time. The city expanded rapidly around all sides of the marsh. Low-priced housing grew up quickly and with it a demand that something be done about the remaining mosquitoes. The cheapest and easiest method of ridding the area of biting flies was to spray with a new miracle called DDT. The area was sprayed at several intervals throughout the summer. The treatment was effective. The flies were killed, and so were crabs and other crustaceans. DDT began to accumulate in the flesh of the fish, until merely to eat a fish from the marsh was likely to destroy the ability of fish-eating birds to reproduce. The heronry on the island had steadily decreased in numbers for a hundred years, but was still active until the spraying program. Then the birds became jumpy and frequently destroyed half completed nests. The eggs were thin-shelled and often infertile. Finally the heronry disappeared altogether.

Although poisoned and drained, the marsh was still a marsh. The tides came and went. *Spartina* continued to grow and small animals, not too much affected by the proximity of humans and resistant enough to survive the dousings of DDT, continued to live in the *Spartina*. Snails throve and climbed the grass stalks at each high tide. Ribbed mussels lived on parts of the marsh low enough to be flooded regularly. They were abundant in the ditches dug to drain the pools, where they were safe from mussel predators. A few raccoons managed to survive, as they were clever enough to avoid men. Ducks still came to the larger creeks during the winter.

In the early 1950's, one of the last Deacons to own the marsh went into partnership with another man and built a marina at the head of a creek. The creek was dredged to increase the size of the basin so that large pleasure boats would anchor. Dredging spoils were dumped on the marsh as fill for an access road and parking. The boats dumped their wastes, without treatment, directly into the water. The water became so polluted that the creeks in the area had to be closed to shellfish taking by the Department of Public Health for the first time.

Sewage from the city was also dumped into the sea, a distance from the marsh, but not so far away that some didn't wash back in with the tides.

Although it was not permitted to take shellfish from the marsh, they grew well in the polluted waters. They were harvested by the state and moved into clean waters to be reharvested and sold two years later. The shellfish were cleaned of the pollution, but they did carry with them the DDT that had been sprayed indiscriminately onto the marsh.

The marsh was dying. Tidal flooding was restricted by a bridge across the bay which reduced the opening to the sea. The water could not flow fast enough to fully flood the marsh, especially at the upper levels. Marsh elder and weeds began to invade the high marsh. Large areas of grass along the creeks were killed when oil slicks from power boats settled on the mud. The areas did not have time to rejuvenate before another slick would settle.

The marina failed but the Deacon family retained title to the property. The house by the marsh was in final decay. It was boarded up and falling apart. The summer colony was now a year-round settlement. The marsh property was finally put up for sale.

A contractor was easily interested in the site for an industrial park. It was close to other industry and the marsh was the last open land in the area. Plans were to fill the marsh, but for that, permission was needed from the Department of Conservation.

The opposition to the filling was led by a local woman. She had enjoyed what she called "the stretch of green ribbon" of the marsh in the past, although now it was nearly spoiled by trash and pollution. She wanted it cleaned up and reinstated as a healthy marsh park. The contractor countered the resistance by stating that his plant would give new taxes and new jobs to the city. And, in any event, the task of reinstating the marsh would be too expensive for the city to undertake.

In the battle between nature and "progress," "progress" won. Permission to fill was granted and the sale went through. The land was first leased to a trash collector from the metropolitan area, who began dumping to fill the marsh the day the agreement was signed. Trash collecting in the city had become a million dollar business. The 1950's and early 60's saw a great increase in the quantities of disposable packaging. Much of the packaging could not be burned and was highly resistant to decay.

Trucks brought trash in a steady stream. Permission to fill stopped short of the creeks and the marsh immediately on their banks, as these were to be preserved for drainage, boat passage, and shellfish production. When the entire area had received one covering of trash, another layer was added.

The filling took considerable time. During this period the marsh was breathing its last. Herring gulls were attracted to the dump in large numbers, although there was little domestic garbage in the fill. They did find enough edible items to keep a large flock busy picking over the rubble. A number of rats moved into the dump but not in the numbers they would have if there had not been the constant rumble of heavy trucks and the difficulty of finding hiding places in the compact fill.

Of the old marsh inhabitants, only the killdeer, never plentiful, made an attempt to stay. The birds used the edge of the fill where active dumping was not current. They even managed to raise a few young although most of the chicks fell victim to the rats and semiwild city cats.

Only the *S. alterniflora* marsh along the creeks was left. It was not healthy and much of it died when oil was accidentally spilled onto the edge of the fill. It killed the plants above and under ground. This turned out to be a minor disaster for the contractor. Without the grass to hold the creek bank in place, it was in danger of washing away. The contractor was required to construct a bulkhead to protect the bank when it became apparent that the grass could not recover.

Filling was finally completed. Construction of the industrial building began with the driving of pilings into the soft substrate. The noise drove the last of the few remaining birds away from the area.

The history of the marsh was over. From birth, after the retreating glacier, to death, under the laws of progress, the marsh had meant much to many. To scores of animal species, it meant life. To the Indians, it meant food. To the first Deacon, it meant open space, a grassland in the wilderness, and sweet ground on which to found a dynasty. To the last Deacon, it meant money.

PART II

Ecology of Salt Marshes

5. Geography and Geology: The Glaciated Coast

THE SALT MARSHES, WHICH LIE ALL ALONG THE EAST coast of North America, begin as grassy arctic marshes in the far north and are followed by marshes tucked in coves and bays along the glaciated coast of the Canadian Maritimes and New England. Very extensive grassy marshes lie behind the barrier beaches of the old, unglaciated mid-Atlantic coast. At their southern limit, the semitropical salt marshes of Florida are taken over by mangrove trees and become salt swamps.

The arctic marshes begin in the northern reaches of Ellesmere Island within the arctic circle, exist on Baffin Island, along the northern shore of Quebec on Hudson Bay, and along the upper reaches of Labrador. These arctic bits of marsh would be a study in themselves. We will limit ourselves to the marshes that occur between the St. Lawrence River and the Gulf of Mexico. These are the marshes with which we are familiar and which may be easily reached from most of our large Eastern cities.

The area from St. Lawrence south to the northern edge of New Jersey, the glaciated coast, retains no evidence of the salt marshes which we know must have existed there before the last ice sheet. The advancing ice obliterated all traces as it pushed southward. The marshes which now exist on this coast have been reestablished since the ice melted.

The first of these marshes, in the north of Nova

Scotia, are small. Here and there are a few pockets of muddy-bottomed land, sufficiently protected from the full force of the bitter north Atlantic winter, and shallow enough to permit the persistent growth of grassy marsh plants. In the protected waters there are small gems of green marsh. They may be as small as a suburban front yard, as one we knew in West Lawrencetown. Lawrencetown also possesses one of the few larger marshes, which may occupy as much as one square mile. None are extensive. But this coast is young and rugged. There has been little time for it to mature since the time the glaciers scraped it clean and the rising sea flooded it. The uplands are composed of hard rock that furnished little sediment to the shore. There has not been time enough for erosion to fill the bays and coves to the level where marsh grasses can survive. On the outer parts of the coast, wave action is severe enough to grind rocks into sand, but the lashings of the rough water will not permit grasses to grow. What sand is allowed to accumulate between the cobbles and boulders during the quiet months of summer is washed away in winter. Time and weather have not favored marshes along this coast.

It is not until as far south as the central coast of Nova Scotia that marshes appear significant. Nova Scotia hangs down into the ocean so that a bay is formed between it and New Brunswick. The shape is such that the mass of water in the bay oscillates naturally in time with the tides. Consequently, the tides are much higher than they would otherwise be. A thirty to fifty foot rise and fall of water is not unusual there.

It is this funnel shape which mothers the wonders of the Bay of Fundy: the reversing falls at St. John's, New Brunswick, and the tidal bores in the rivers at the heads of the bay. The incoming waters in the new tidal wave abruptly steepen when they run into the narrow, relatively shallow river mouths and meet the outgoing river waters. The steep tidal wave reaches its breaking point

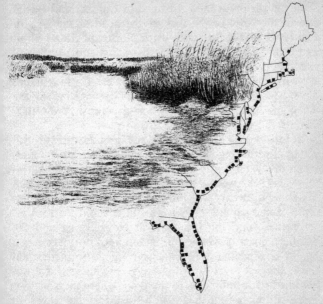

Principal salt marshes along East Coast

and gives the uninitiated viewer the amazing spectacle of a low waterfall moving upstream in the riverbed.

A large amount of water rushes in and out of the rivers at the heads of the Bay of Fundy with each tide. This rush of water has deeply scoured the red sandstones from which the bay was cut and gives a reddish color to the whole area. Extensive salt marshes flourish along the shores at the heads of the bay (there are two, split like the tines of a fork with a tongue of land between). The roiling tides dump large amounts of sand and silt on the flats of which the grasses are quick to take advantage. Even these marshes look red from scoured sandstone wherever the grass is thin enough for the soil to show through.

In the region around the head of Cumberland Basin, one of the tines of the fork at the head of the Bay of Fundy which reaches up toward Northumberland Strait and Prince Edward Island, there are fifty square miles of salt marsh and diked salt marsh, including the well-known marshes of the Tantramar River. These marshes have been diked since the time of Evangeline of the Acadians, and are still used for growing hay, as they were in those historic days.

Before the dikes were built, at high tide the purplish water covered eight-five square miles. Six hours later, when the water had completed its rush out of the basin, there lay exposed about fifty square miles of green marsh and twenty square miles of reddish mud flat. Only fifteen square miles were still covered with water.

Farther south on the coast of Nova Scotia and the northern coast of Maine, the situation of northern Nova Scotia is repeated. The extensive inlets, formed when the rising sea level drowned the river valleys, have not yet filled with sediments to the point where marshes can form. Enough time has not passed for the waves to grind enough sand to seal off the mouths of these drowned valleys with sandbars. Without the protecting bay-mouth bars, there is poor chance for what little fine silt and clay is brought down from the uplands by rivers to settle near shore. The fine particles travel out to the quiet deep water in the Gulf of Maine before many chance to settle out on the bottom. Even up in the protected parts of the inlets, there has not often been enough accumulation of material to make the water shallow enough for marsh to arise. The marshes resemble the bits and pieces to the far north.

In neither place can the muds and grasses get together in a sufficiently protected spot to form a sizable marsh. At Bath, Maine, and the mouth of the Kennebec River, there is a nice little outcropping of marshes. Scarboro has a beautiful marsh bordered by woods. But large marshes do not occur until New Hampshire and Newburyport, Massachusetts, are reached.

Marshes totaling over twenty square miles occupy the areas behind the barrier beaches of Hampton Beach and Plum Island and in the mouth of the Merrimack River and along the Parker River and its tributaries.

The Parker River is a tidal river which carries seawater in and out rather than a drainage river which carries freshwater to the sea. At one time there was a bay where the river is now. A few small streams entered it from the surrounding uplands. There was a plentiful supply of sand in the area left by the glacier. This sand, moved by sea waves and upland streams, made protective bars and shallows. Marshes gradually filled the bay. The Parker River is a bit of the old bay still kept open by the tidal currents that run in or out each six hours. South of this, in the Massachusetts Bay area, eight to eleven foot tides cover and uncover large areas of marsh.

The Massachusetts Bay area contains the great marshes in Saugus and Revere, the marshes of Quincy, and the smaller marshes of Hingham and Cohasset. Farther south are extensive marshes that gave the name to Marshfield. The North River, which changes from fresh to salt as you approach the sea, winds leisurely through these wetlands. Canoeing here is a delight.

Salt marshes exist along the rest of the Massachusetts coast, at Duxbury south of Marshfield, on Cape Cod at Barnstable and on the lower Cape, and along the shores of Buzzards Bay. Spotted in bays and behind protective bars, they occur all along the southern New England coast from southern Massachusetts through Rhode Island and Connecticut.

On the south shore of Long Island, marshes occur which are very important to waterfowl migrating along the Eastern flyway. The westernmost of these in Jamaica Bay are within the boundaries of New York City, as are the Pelham and Staten Island marshes. These areas are heavily polluted and certainly the least attractive along the coast. The waters which feed many of them are iridescent with oily wastes which leave the mud and plants black, poisoned by detergents, and defiled by massive loads of sewage. There are still areas in the city where the marshes give a hint of their former glory. But lack of concern for nature has robbed us of much of this once magnificent marsh.

The marshes to this point were formed on land scraped bare by the ice or on new land created by the piles of debris left by retreating ice. Regardless of where they formed, they have common characteristics. They grow two types of grass, each in its preferred area. *Spartina alterniflora*, also called thatch or cord grass, grows three to six feet tall along the twisting creeks and seaward edges of the marsh. *Spartina patens*, salt hay grass, gives its fine texture to the higher, more landward parts of the marsh. *S. alterniflora* marshes are bright green in summer. The grass washes away in winter, leaving only a stubble which reveals the surface of the marsh. The *S. patens* marshes retain the brown cover of grass throughout winter. In early summer, the brown cover is supplanted by the pale green shoots of young plants.

The histories of these marshes of the glaciated portion of our coast are similar. They were molded from the same events and climactic occurrences which accompanied the melting of the ice after the last of several glaciations.

Periods of semitropical heat alternated with periods of great cold, with a broad spectrum of changes between, during the ice age. At times, when the earth was warmer than at present, there was less ice on the land. The level of the seas, containing water now locked in the ice caps of Antarctica and Greenland, was higher than it is now. If these remnants of the great glaciers were to melt, the level of the oceans would rise about one hundred feet, drowning many of the most populated regions of the world.

At other times during the ice ages, the climate was colder than at present and ice, as much as two miles thick in the center, spread from Hudson Bay down into

Iowa and Ohio, and buried New York and New England. The sea level was much lower because water from the sea was frozen into the great ice caps. At periods of maximum ice, men and animals then living could walk out for a hundred miles over lands that now lie at the bottom of the ocean.

Under the massive glacier, the land sank, and the ice-free land next to it tilted up. When the ice melted, about ten thousand years ago, the land that had been weighted down gradually rose toward its former position and the adjacent land sank again. Sea level changed in both areas. But the most important process in change in sea level was the addition of water to the oceans from the melting ice. As the ice melted, the sea rose all along the coast.

The coastline was progressively flooded. River valleys became estuaries. Islands became shoals and high points of peninsulas became islands. It is only in the last half of the ten thousand year period since the retreat of the last ice cap that our present salt marshes could have formed.

Spartina seeds germinate best in areas where the water is fresher than it is in the sea. They germinate best on mud and sand flats where the seawater is diluted by rains or by freshwater coming into the sea at the mouth of a stream or river. Some of the seeds will germinate in seawater after a month or two of soaking, but most will germinate within two weeks in freshwater. There is nothing harmful about seawater to the seeds but sea salts prevent the seeds from soaking up enough water to promote growth. If seeds soaking in seawater are transferred to freshwater, they will germinate readily.

Spartina seedlings cannot compete successfully with other plants that can live in freshwater marshes. If the area is fresh enough for these plants, *Spartina* is very likely to be crowded out before it really gets started, and a *Spartina* marsh cannot develop. The area must be fresher than seawater for *Spartina* seeds to germinate readily in large numbers, but it must be saltier than freshwater if a *Spartina* marsh is to grow.

Once the *Spartina* colonized a suitable area in times past, it brought about changes that accelerated the development of the salt marsh. The changes were greatest where *Spartina* germinated on a sand flat, slightly above the mid-tide level in a protected cover. There the seedling thrived and grew quickly. Like all good turf-forming grasses, it began to send out underground stems, rhizomes. Further sprouts began to appear on all sides of the original seedling. Soon the stems formed a clump of grass plants. They slowed the tidal currents that flowed among them and caused the water to drop a portion of the sediment it was carrying. The sand and mud began to accumulate around the stems. The level of the marsh rose. As the process continued, the old rhizomes and roots of the grasses contributed to the accumulation of material. The grass spread farther away from its original center.

The flooding tides dropped sand and other coarse material at the edges of the marsh. Only fine mud was left to settle out in the center. The surface of the original bit of marsh changed from sandy to a mixture of mud and plant remains, a muddy peat.

The marsh level rose more slowly in the areas that were isolated from the tidal currents by the spread of the grass. The supply of sediment brought in by the water lessened and lessened the farther the water moved into the grass, and the flow became even slower. *Spartina* itself slowed in growth in the regions away from the tidal currents, for reasons we will consider later, and so the accumulation of plant material was also slowed.

In some of these central areas, the growth became so slow that the surrounding marsh grew up and diked them in. Once this occurred, water that flooded the area at high tide was trapped and remained throughout the low tide period. *Spartina* is a most hardy plant, but it cannot survive in standing water. Such dished areas became pools on the salt marsh. The grass roots and rhizomes rotted away and some of the silt and clay floated out. The pool deepened. If the pool was formed early in the growth of the marsh, the deepening stopped when a firm sandy bottom was reached. Ruppia, called widgeon grass, which lives with its tops as well as its roots always underwater, invades such pools.

In other adjacent areas, the growth of the marsh was sufficient to raise it to high tide level. At this level, the marsh is flooded by about half of the high tides and remains exposed during the other half. Less material is brought onto the surface by the tides and growth in height of the marsh is slowed. *Spartina alterniflora* does not grow as well here, and is usually much shorter than that growing a few feet away near the creeks. The plants are more widely spaced, also, and other marsh plants occasionally grow in between the *Spartina* plants.

Sequence of stages of marsh group

When a point about a foot higher is reached, the marsh growth comes to a standstill, a stalemate with the tides. There is no longer enough flooding to carry appreciable amounts of sediment onto the marsh surface to raise the ground level. Only the spring tides cover the ground, that is, the highest tides. At this level, *Spartina patens* grows better than does *Spartina alterniflora*, and takes over the surface of the marsh. But if the marsh level rises more than about one foot above mean high tide level, the growth of *Spartina patens* is reduced. With less plant material added to the marsh surface each year, the balance between accumulation and decomposition of the peat is shifted toward the latter. The level of the marsh is reduced slightly until the grass can again grow well.

Sometimes on the high marsh, just as on the lower elevations, an area will become waterlogged. Drainage will be blocked by differential marsh growth or perhaps by the chance deposition of a dam of material left by ice, tides, or human activities. The *Spartina*, with its roots continuously underwater, dies and the peat decomposes. But in an area where the peat is deep, such a rotten spot cannot form the same sort of pool as is found on lower levels of the marsh. It develops into what is called a pond hole. The composition of the bottom of the pond hole is quite different from other marsh pools. It is composed of firm peat in the beginning, but as this peat bottom rots, it gets softer and softer. The bottom of a well-developed pond hole is like quicksand in consistency. It looks firm but there is little support for anything heavier than water.

The water in these pond holes may vary in salinity as it is concentrated by evaporation during dry periods and diluted by rains during wet. The same variations occur to the water in the pools in lower areas of marsh, but there it is changed twice a day by the tides and so does not vary much from local seawater.

Most of the plants in the pond holes are algae. Often a mat of green or blue-green algae covers the bottom. On a bright sunny day the mat is covered with tiny bubbles of oxygen produced by algal photosynthesis. These bubbles may eventually float the mat to the surface of the pool during the day. At night when bubble production is stopped by darkness, the mat sinks to the bottom again. It is small wonder that the pond holes, with their varying salinity, indistinct bottom, and poor connection with the sea, have a quite different sort of life in them than other parts of the marsh.

Since they are above the level at which tides could bring sediment to fill them, pond holes may have a very long life. Some may be drained by the headward erosion of a creek into the pond hole. When this happens, the trapped water is released. Other than this erosion, there is little to change pond holes unless they are drained artificially.

Pools may also form near land where peat is very shallow. These pools extend to the sand underlying the peat. They have a firm bottom and highly variable salinity. They may dry up completely at times during the summer.

Aside from occasional formation or destruction of a pool, the high marsh is stable, its level determined by a balance between tides, plant growth, compaction of the underlying peat, and erosion.

At least, we might suppose that such a process would occur if this whole simple picture of the growth of a salt marsh were not complicated by two other processes that have already been mentioned: the changes in sea level that have occurred throughout the period of salt marsh growth; and the erosive action of wind and water that continually transports sand and silt about on the surface of the earth.

Sediment is the material which builds up the bottom of the shallow seas, making the area ready for *Spartina* seedlings to begin growth there. It settles onto the surface and helps, with the accumulated remains of dead plants, to build up the surface of the marsh. Sediment is continually being removed from the land as a result of the erosion of the surface by the winds and waters that blow and flow over it. Some of the eroded material is carried by the winds and falls out as dust all over the surface of the oceans. But by far the greater part is removed by flowing water and is eventually washed down the rivers into the seas.

Erosion from the land in New England is not very great. The hard rocks of the uplands are not easily weathered and eroded. Even where soils are bare of plant cover, they tend to be sandy. Water filters through them rather than running off along the surface and carries soil with it. Erosion was no doubt severe just as the glaciers were retreating, when enormous quantities of water were running to the sea and plant cover was minimal. There was no mulch of dead plant parts to protect the soils and there was much subsoil frost to retard downward percolation of water. But the soils thawed completely and plants colonized them rapidly. When they did, erosion dropped to present low levels.

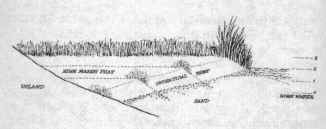

Marsh development
along shore, showing effect of rising sea level

Once erosion from the land diminished, most of the sediments on which the salt marshes have grown was brought into the coves and bays, not by the rivers which enter them at their heads, but by the tides entering at their mouths. The tidal cycle is such that the velocity of flow is generally greater during rising tide than during the fall. Faster flowing water can carry more sediment. The flooding tide carries more sand into the coves and bays than the slower ebb can remove. Sediment accumulates and the marsh can grow out into what was deeper water.

The history of the growth of a New England marsh has been best studied in the case of Barnstable Marsh on Cape Cod. By noting the depth of the peat and its relation to the underlying sand and shores, Dr. Alfred Redfield of Woods Hole, Massachusetts, has traced the history of this marsh from its formation about four thousand years ago.

Barnstable Marsh came into being when the sea level was eighteen to twenty feet lower than it is now. *Spartina alterniflora* colonized the shores of a shallow indentation along the north shore of Cape Cod. The action of the waves had first cut a cliff into a sandy hill that rose along the shore. This cliff still rises above the top of the marsh, although its base is buried deep within the accumulated peat.

Soon after the cliff was cut, the sand, moved by the waves, began to form a spit which grew parallel to the general line of the shore. The spit grew across the opening of the indentation which now contains the marsh and Barnstable Harbor.

All of the conditions necessary for the growth of a marsh were then present. There were suitable intertidal flats on which *Spartina* could get a healthy start, trap sediment, and produce an accumulation of salt marsh peat. There was a slowly rising sea level which enabled the marsh to grow in depth. A steady supply of sediment was continuously added to the spit and filled in the central parts of the harbor. This increased the protected area in which the marsh could survive and enabled it to spread into the harbor from the edges.

Spartina alterniflora did its usual work of building up the marsh until it reached a level above the average high tide, when *S. patens* replaced it. The marsh now fills the upper portions of the harbor and has developed to the stage where ninety percent of it is flat high marsh lying at high tide level to about one foot above. Stunted *Spartina alterniflora* grows over most of the area, with *Spartina patens* occurring on the higher and older parts. Intertidal, tall *S. alterniflora* is left only along the tidal creeks. There is no further filling of the creek areas for they have achieved a balance between deposition and erosion. The amount of water that must flow through the creeks to flood the marsh at high tide cannot be contained in smaller channels. Although the creek channels may change their position somewhat, their overall

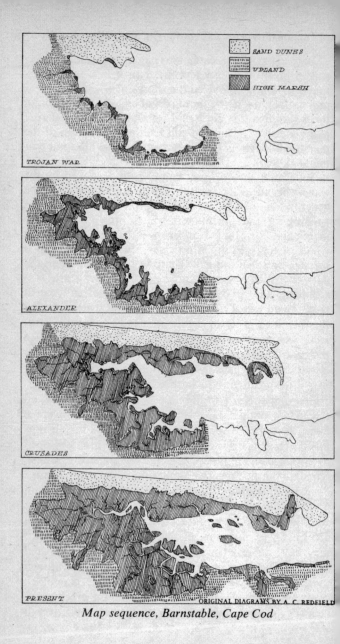

SAND DUNES
UPLAND
HIGH MARSH

TROJAN WAR

ALEXANDER

CRUSADES

PRESENT

ORIGINAL DIAGRAMS BY A. C. REDFIELD

Map sequence, Barnstable, Cape Cod

size is fixed by the volume of tidal water they must carry.

As the sea level rose and the marsh grew in height, it also spread over what had been the edge of the upland. Under high marsh peat are the remains of meadows, forests, and freshwater marshes along the streams. Farther out into the marsh, the high marsh peat is underlaid by intertidal *S. alterniflora* peat, which can be distinguished by its greater amount of sand and lesser water content as well as the coarser plant remains in it. The intertidal peat in turn rests upon the sand that once formed the bottom of the harbor. The peat is deepest at a point where the shoreline existed when the marsh began, and thinnest at both edges where it is still growing out onto the harbor sand flats and up onto the surrounding uplands.

There are visible remains of shipping activities centered in the marsh. A transport road runs to what was the upper limit of navigation. The remains of a boat ramp lie buried under a foot of peat. They are exposed at one edge where the cut for a modern boat ramp was made. Men now slip their crafts over mud where they used to haul over a stone and log ramp.

Once a marsh basin has filled, as it has in many of the coves along the southern New England coast, development is slowed. As sea level continues to rise, the marsh keeps pace. It grows somewhat in area as the rising sea level permits the marsh grasses to encroach on the surrounding land. The larger tidal creeks develop strong currents when they are carrying maximum water necessary to flood the entire high marsh area. They cut into the creek banks wherever they bend, cutting and eroding them on the outside of the bends. Mud is deposited on the inside of the bends, which is then invaded by *S. alterniflora*. The peat is not easily eroded, however, and the meander pattern of the creeks, formed when they were young, is quite unchanged in the present marshes.

This picture would be a good likeness to any New

England or Canadian maritime marsh. The differences between marshes are mainly a matter of time scale. In southern New England where the glaciers dumped their sediment and in the Bay of Fundy where the rocks are soft and easily eroded, there has been much sedimentation.

The deposition of the abundant sand and silts kept up with the rising sea level, and the sheltered bays and coves have stayed shallow enough for the marshes to move ever farther out into what used to be water. But in the other parts of this glaciated coast, the sediment supply was limited. The glaciers scraped the loose material from Maine and left it out on George's Bank and from the Atlantic shore of Nova Scotia and left it where Sable Island and the fishing banks are now located. The rocks exposed in both these places are hard and do not erode easily. There has been too little sediment to fill in the bays and coves and they are still, in large measure, too deep for successful *Spartina* development. In the normal course of the world, these bays will also fill with marsh. But this will not happen until long after we are gone from the shore.

6. Geography and Geology: The Unglaciated Coast

FROM NEW JERSEY SOUTH, INDIVIDUAL SALT MARSHES are much more extensive than along the glaciated coast to the north. Here the ribbon of green extends almost the entire length of the coast, broken naturally only by great estuaries and the many rivers that drain into the sea. The strip of marshes is also artificially broken by the activities of men who fill, dredge, and drain.

Where the marshes are undisturbed, they flourish. Barrier beaches swarming with sun worshippers, barrier islands studded with vacation houses, and Delaware Bay protect about three hundred and fifty square miles of salt marsh in New Jersey. The Cape May marshes are well known for the millions of shorebirds and waterfowl attracted during migrations and during the winter season.

Most of the New Jersey marshes, flooded only at the highest high and storm tides, grow fine salt hay, *S. patens*. In days past, large quantities of this hay have been cut and some is still cut, especially on the marshes along Delaware Bay.

The western side of Delaware Bay is rich in extensive marshes. Large areas have been incorporated in Bombay Hook and Prime Hook National Wildlife Refuges. This part of the Bay shows more growth of *Spartina alterniflora* than does the New Jersey side. Still, extensive areas of *S. patens* grow on high marshes.

The biggest break in the coastal ribbon of marshes is caused by Chesapeake Bay. Marshes are especially abundant along the islands and bays of the eastern shore. The western side of the Bay is relatively poor in salt marshes, and those to the northward end of the Bay have been filled to a large extent.

From Albemarle Sound on the coast of North Carolina south to the northern coast of Florida, salt marshes are found in their greatest abundance. Thousands of square miles between the coastal plain and the barrier beaches and islands are covered with marsh grasses.

The marshes bordering Pamlico Sound, which has a relatively small tide, grow most *S. patens*, as do those to the north. But from near Beaufort Inlet south, the marshes show a different character. Tides are higher and flood a greater area of marsh with daily regularity. Large level meadows of *S. patens* are missing. Flat areas, as well as creek banks, are covered by *S. alterniflora*, while the *S. patens* occur as a narrow band along the upland edge of the marsh, if at all. Grass on the upper parts of the marsh is short and sparse, and muddy soil and animals show through. Plant growth along the creeks is tall and lush. A new type of marsh, covered with a coarse black rush, *Juncus roemerianus*, makes its appearance, especially in areas of some freshwater inflow. The southeastern marshes do not have as many small ponds on their surface as do the more northern marshes. Drainage patterns of tidal creeks and rivers are more fully developed. These marshes of the North Carolina, South Carolina, and Georgia coasts give sport to large numbers of hunters and fishermen.

The far-reaching marshes described by Sidney Lanier, 1842–1881, in his poem "The Marshes of Glynn" constitute one of the most productive coastal areas in the world. They are viewed by thousands of visitors who cross them to visit Georgia's sea islands.

Marshes extend down into northern Florida, but finally in the far south, the mangroves take over from the grasses. The narrow creeks are hidden by a mangrove canopy and the interfingering of land and sea, so characteristic of northern marshes, is invisible from above. Forest runs to the edge of the sea where the two meet in an uneven scalloped border. Some of the most magnificent mangrove forests in the world form the southern end of our ribbon of green.

The history of these marshes and swamps of the region, never visited by the great glaciers, has been somewhat different from that of those to the north. The coast was subject to great changes in sea level due to the locking up of water in ice and subsequent melting, but it did not have the added burden of being pressed down by the ice. The cover of soils and sands was never scraped away and there are few rocks exposed on the coast.

Differences in the geology of the coast, as well as the differences in glacial history, affected marsh development. The part of the East Coast with the greatest runoff in rivers is to the north. Omitting the St. Lawrence River, which is five times as big as the next largest East Coast river, the rivers carrying most water to the sea are the Susquehanna, entering at the head of Chesapeake Bay; the St. John, rising in Maine and flowing through New Brunswick, Canada; the Hudson, flowing into New York harbor; the Delaware, which widens into Delaware Bay; and the Connecticut, which enters Long Island Sound at Old Lyme after flowing straight down through New England.

These rivers carry large amounts of water. Rainfall is high and the ground is generally not very porous in the north. Seepage is limited. When the continental glaciers were melting, these rivers carried even more water than they do now. They then cut the great valleys, later flooded by the rising sea level, which form New York harbor, Delaware and Chesapeake Bays.

While the rivers carrying the most water flow in the wet, hard-rock north, those carrying the greatest sediment load flow through the softrock uplands of the south. The Santee of South Carolina, the Altamaha and the Savannah of Georgia, the Roanoke rising in Virginia and entering the sea in Albemarle Sound, North Carolina, and the Pee Dee rising in North Carolina and entering the sea in South Carolina carry the greatest sediment loads.

Although a lot of rain falls in this southwest region, much seeps into the ground and moves through the porous rocks to the sea. Less water is left to flow down the rivers. But the porous rocks and the soils formed from them are easily eroded and the smaller amount of water in the rivers carries a much greater amount of silt and sand. One reason there are no great estuaries, like the Delaware and Chesapeake farther south, is that the rivers brought enough sediment to fill their valleys as they were being flooded by rising sea level.

It is very difficult to guess the rate of erosion before Europeans entered North America. No one was interested in measuring land loss in the early days of our country before the land was disturbed by plowing, grazing, road building, and all the other disrupting actions to which civilized men subject the land.

There are some recent measurements made on uplands which have been cut over but are now reforested. Such land on the uplands at the eastern side of the Appalachians in the Virginia-Pennsylvania region, where the rocks are of the sedimentary type, loses twenty-five tons of soil from each square mile each year to the streams that drain it. We may suppose that the flatter lands between these mountains and the sea lose less soil, as do the harder rock areas to the north of the country.

With this sediment, the salt marsh muds were built up slowly over the years. Rivers and streams robbed the uplands, bringing rich soils to the sea. The soils were trapped in the estuaries and provided new ground on which salt-resistant plants could grow.

Erosion was proceeding naturally. Then with the arrival of Europeans to North America, it took a tremendous spurt upward. When the early explorers wrote about the rivers of the eastern seaboard, they wrote of clear streams and clean waters. Father White wrote of the Potomac in 1630, "This is the sweetest and greatest river I have seene. . . . There are noe marshes or swampes about it, but solid firme ground. . . ."

In 1711, Baron de Graffenried, a colonial leader, selected an angle between Rock Creek and the Potomac River as one suitable for settlement because there one could sail vessels into the bay and find ample room for anchorage.

Joppatown, Maryland, was founded in 1707 at the spot where the waters of two relatively small rivers met: the Chesapeake and the Gunpowder Arm. Hundreds of other towns were founded in similar situations to serve as shipping ports for the heavy hogsheads of tobacco from nearby farms.

Growing tobacco for the ever increasing demand in the mother country had a tremendous effect on the land, on the ports, and on the marshes along the coast. No effort was made to care for the land, to prevent rain from washing the soil away, and to plant cover crops to protect the soil during winter. As soon as a field was exhausted by repetitious planting of the crop, the tobacco grower cleared another field and abandoned the first to nature. In the early days there was no shortage of land. As far as the colonists were concerned, there were new fields to clear forever.

Erosion, so slight before settlement that the rivers were clear to the eyes of the colonists, increased in amount and the rivers assumed their present muddy appearance as the poorly managed fields lost their topsoil to the waters. At first, the waters were muddy only after heavy rains or great storms. Then they became steadily and increasingly murky.

Rivers can carry an enormous amount of mud from the land to the sea in a few days. They can appear only slightly murky most of the time, and still carry enough mud to fill large areas of coastal waters. For actual figures we must move up to the present time when measurements have been made.

The Delaware River, carrying its runoff from a relatively narrow basin in eastern Pennsylvania and western New Jersey, now carries about one million tons of sediments to the sea every year. Twice in the last two decades, after a hurricane, the Delaware carried one million tons of sediment to the sea in only one day. On the average, for the last fifty years, the river carried ten percent of its load in less than two days, and one quarter of its load in only thirty days. Half of the entire erosion of fifty years was carried to the sea on days after storms that amount to a total time of less than six months. The fact that today or tomorrow the river is not very muddy says almost nothing about the amount of material that is being transported to the sea.

A study of the Potomac River shows that it is carrying two and one half million tons of sediment per year on the average, or one hundred seventy tons from each square mile of its drainage basin. The basin includes much forested country from which erosion is slight.

From an average rural square mile in the piedmont, the foot of the mountains, the river annually carries off two hundred to four hundred tons of sediment. From land that is completely under cultivation, it removes five hundred to one thousand tons. During the period when the rural land is being changed to urban developments, the river receives no less than ten thousand tons of soil from each square mile every year. Probably some fifty thousands tons are removed during the transition from rural to urban, which is equivalent to about one half inch of soil from the entire square mile.

The areas of shallow coastal waters are very small in comparison to the vast continental areas from which the rivers get their sediment. Even if the removal of that vast amount of material from the land has not greatly affected the geography of the continent since the coming of the Europeans, there has been a noticeable effect on the coastline.

Joppatown was built on the edge of a bay in which oceangoing merchant ships anchored. Soon after being founded in 1707, it became the county seat and most important port in Maryland. But erosion from the new farms began to fill the port immediately. The town and shipping began to decline by 1750, and eighteen years later the county seat was moved to Baltimore, twenty miles away, where shipping had easier access to deep water. Today you must walk two miles from the old stone mooring posts at Joppatown before coming to the edge of navigable waters. Where ships once anchored at Gunpowder Arm, marshes and forests now exist.

Baltimore was founded a year before Joppatown, although the town of Elk Ridge was the first port at that site, about seven miles upstream from the Hanover Street bridge, at the limit of the tidewater. But even early in the eighteenth century, Elk Ridge could no longer serve as a port.

There were seventeen feet of water at the Hanover Street bridge in 1845, three and a half feet in 1898, and only six inches in 1924. The basin at the southern side of Baltimore harbor, the basin that was the passage to that first harbor at Elk Ridge, is now completely filled in. Of the hundreds of ports founded at the limits of navigation to serve the tobacco farmers, all but one was destroyed by the farmers' agricultural methods. Baltimore survives only by ceaseless dredging.

The Potomac Bays, looked upon so favorably by Baron de Graffenried, were silted up, became marshes, and were finally filled. Lincoln Memorial in Washington, D.C., now stands where ships once anchored. Maryland alone has gained hundreds of acres of territory by unwittingly using her topsoil to fill in her coastline.

The principal beneficiary of all this erosional activity has been the salt marsh. Animals and plants that lived in the old estuaries were buried and suffocated under a blanket of mud which eventually became thick enough to reach up to mid-tide level where salt marsh plants invaded the new area.

Salt marshes can also be destroyed by this process of erosion. While the tide cannot build a marsh up above high tide level, a river flood can. The high river waters, loaded with extra amounts of silt characteristic of flood waters, can overspread a marsh, bury it in mud, and leave the level above tides so that marsh changes into a freshwater swamp or forest. New marshes are formed and destroyed at river mouths now, at a rate faster than ever before.

Not all marshes are near river mouths. Those which are not are less affected by increased speed of erosion from the land. In such areas you can see the history of salt marshes as influenced by only normal sediment gains and by the changes in sea level, a more natural picture of salt marsh development.

Along the southern shores of the Atlantic coast, the effect of the changes in sea level throughout the ice ages has been to move the surf alternately up onto the land and out on the continental shelf. With these changes, marshes have had the opportunity to develop at several levels. Some below the present sea level can be seen by diving, but you can look, dry-shod, at several ancient marshes that are left high and dry above those of the present sea level.

These old marshes are associated with the old beach ridges that can be followed on the coastal plain running parallel to the present beach. They are hidden by the plants and soils that have developed atop them after the salts were leached out, but they can be identified by digging into them or finding them exposed in road cuts. From New Jersey to Georgia, at least two can still be seen behind the old dunes which were the barrier islands at the time the old marshes were alive. They can be noticed by the rather sudden rise of ten to twenty feet in a roadbed where it passes over the old beach dunes.

The ancient barrier islands, like the present ones, were formed as the sea level rose in times of warming climate. As the sea rose, it carried sand with it. During

Development of shoreline

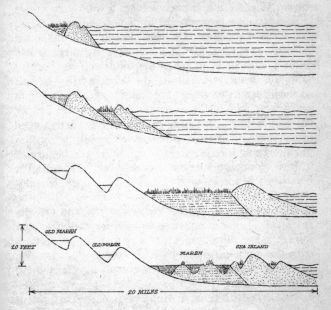

OLD MARSH

20 FEET

OLD MARSH

OLD MARSH

MARSH

SEA ISLAND

20 MILES

periods of relative stability, this sand was pushed by waves and wind into dunes such as can now be found along beaches. In some way, perhaps a slight decrease in sea level accompanied by erosion, a shallow valley formed behind the dunes. This filled with salt marsh during the last stages of rising sea level at each of these stable periods.

It might seem that we are asking for an almost impossible coincidence between rise in sea level and rate of plant growth so that the marsh will just be able to keep up with the water. But it really isn't coincidence. If the rise in sea level is slower, the rise in the surface of the marsh will be slower or temporarily stop. If sea level rises slightly faster than the plant growth can add to the surface of the marsh, the surface will be flooded more frequently with sediment-laden waters. The accumulation of mud on the surface will increase and keep the marsh level in harmony with sea level.

The balance between sea level and marsh level may extend to slight lowerings of the sea as well. If the high tides do not flood the marsh regularly, there will be periods without rains when the mud will dry out. The salinity will increase, due to the concentration of salts, as the water evaporates. The marsh plants will die and no longer hold the mud in place. Subsequent rains or extra high tides will reduce the level of the marsh again, by increased erosion, until it is about at the level of mean high tide.

It is common to find this kind of balance struck between the forces of the environment and the plants that live in that environment, each modifying the effects of the other. It is only at periods of rapidly changing sea level, during continental ice cap formation or melting, that the development of a marsh cannot keep up with the changes in sea level. At these times, marshes are either buried by the rising waters or left high and dry on the land.

It was at the time of formation of the last ice cap that the elevated beach ridges and their associated salt marshes were abandoned by the sea. It was after the retreat of the ice, when sea level changes had slowed after their initial rapid rise due to melting of the great glaciers, that the present marshes were formed behind the present sea islands running from New Jersey to north Florida.

Most of the present sea islands were also the sea islands of the period just before the last ice advance. The sea level at that time had already left the elevated beach ridges behind and had been apparently stabilized for a long time at a level two or three feet higher than at present. The coastline must have looked then much as it does now everywhere south of the limits of glaciation. When the continental glaciers grew, so much water was trapped as ice that the sea level fell throughout the world. The marshes behind the islands were much eroded as the marsh plants died.

It happened that, when the glaciers melted and sea level rose again, erosion slowed to a rate which allowed marsh development to keep up with it at about the level of the bottom of the old eroded marsh. The area was again filled with salt marsh. The only difference between the old coastline and the present one is that the rising sea brought some new sand and added slightly to the sea islands. In Georgia where it is best illustrated, there is now a new beach ridge separated from the main mass of the sea islands by a narrow salt marsh.

This is the present situation along the coast of Georgia as it has been discovered by geologists working at the marine laboratory on Sapelo Island.

A similar sequence of sea level changes must have occurred in Florida, but the materials on which the moving waters worked were quite different. Mangroves grow along the shore instead of *Spartina* grasses. The rocks above which they grow are limestone instead of the thick layers of sand on top of soft rocks found farther north. The elevated beaches are visible in places. The main group of Florida Keys is the emerged string of offshore barrier coral reefs that formed during the period of the highest beach ridge. The recent rise in sea level is indicated by the mangrove peat, eight to ten feet deep, that lies under the present mangrove swamp.

The shape of the Florida shoreline is often scalloped, a result of resting on a limestone base. Limestone is easily dissolved by slightly acid-ground water. Rain falling on forest or field picks up acid plant decay products, seeps into the porous rock, and dissolves out caverns. These cavities often collapse, leaving the sinkhole typical of a limestone topography. In Florida, the rising sea flooded a coastal area pockmarked with intersecting pits. The mangroves could grow along the slightly submerged edges but have seldom been able to colonize the deeper water in the center of the pits.

The marshes of the unglaciated coast have been subject to a number of conditions that have changed them during the long years of their existence.

Some of the barrier islands are very unsubstantial, nothing more than a row of dunes and beach protecting the marsh from the onslaughts of the sea. Sometimes circumstances combine to remove the barriers. The supplies of sand may be removed from the beach by along-shore currents. Onshore winds may drive the dunes back onto the marsh. If these processes are combined, large sections of marsh may be destroyed.

Red mangrove

The marsh is first buried by the sand and suffocated. It is later reexposed as the dunes move farther inland and remaining sand is carried off by the currents. The peat erodes at rates that vary depending on hardness. It may wash away almost immediately if it is the soft, soupy sort, but it may be more resistant than the sand if it is firm and well bound together with roots. Even if it is resistant, it will wash away within a few years and a new opening into the marsh-estuarine area behind the barrier beach will be created.

Remains of the old marsh often persist for hundreds and thousands of years once they have been worn down to where they are deep enough so that they are not much affected by breaking waves. They can be seen as peat beds by divers exploring the floor of the sea.

Though these new openings in the barrier beaches separating the marshes and sea are continually made, there is no total decrease in the extent of the barrier. The sand and sediment removed in the process of opening a new hole are transferred along the coast. Old channels are filled in and closed above as often as new ones are opened. When an old channel stops up, the barrier so constructed protects the waters in back of itself and a new marsh develops to replace the one destroyed elsewhere up or down the shore.

The flow of water in the marsh creeks and rivers also changes the marsh continually. While there is evidence that the general course of marsh creeks in the northern marshes has not changed appreciably during their entire existence, this is not the case in more southern marshes. There the peat is soft, called muck rather than peat in many cases. It does not resist the eroding effects of the tidal waters, and meanders in the creeks become more and more exaggerated until they become so extreme that two bends meet. The old channel is cut off, leaving an oxbow segment of creek which soon fills with mud and is reclaimed by *Spartina*. Considerable areas of some marshes show evidence in the peat of such reworking of the sediments by wandering tidal creeks.

Along the coast where the rivers bring a heavy load of sediment to the sea, the waters of the marshes are themselves heavily laden with silt. As the waters rush along, they spill over the bends at high water. The flow is suddenly slowed, both because of the much larger area into which the water moves and because of friction with the dense grass stems. As the water is abruptly checked, it loses much of its sediment load until, eventually, a raised area is built along the creek. As the levee grows still higher, there are longer and longer periods between floodings and greater and greater chance that the mud will dry out.

The plants living behind the levees begin to suffer from increased salinity. Oxygen penetrates into the mud where it oxidizes the sulfides waiting below the surface and converts them to sulfates. In ordinary muds, the sulfates are quite harmless, but in certain "cat clays" found in many southern marshes, the sulfates appear in the form of sulfuric acid. When acid forms, all vegetation is killed. Where this disaster strikes, the affected levee muds are rapidly eroded as they then have no binding root mat to hold them in place. The marsh returns to an earlier state and begins to evolve again.

In some marshes that have been diked and drained for agriculture, restricted by man-made levees impervious to erosion, it is years before the acids are leached out of the soils and the ground made sweet for crops.

Salt marshes are dynamic features of the coastal landscape. They grow in size depending on the rate of plant growth and the supply of sediment. They adjust to changes in sea level. They tend to fill their basins a little above that of mean high tide and maintain that level, adding new peat as the old settles and compacts beneath the growing plants.

Marshes occasionally lose a bit of area to the land. Near river mouths or behind windswept sandy beaches, enough sediment might accumulate on top of the marsh to permit rains to wash away the salt and land plants to grow. But only two events really destroy salt marshes at the present moment in history.

In a few places, the wave action may erode the protective barrier beaches. The surf pounding on the soft marsh muds will then quickly wash them away. New inlets and coves can form. This process may even be accelerated by a great storm and occur overnight.

The other agency which can destroy marshes is man with his massive dredge and filling tools. Man will certainly determine the future of all coastal salt marshes.

And quite soon.

7. The Dominant "*Spartinas*"

THE MARSH IS DEFINED BY THE KINDS OF PLANTS which grow on it. They are responsible for the very existence of these wetlands but the number of species is limited. The marsh environment is hostile to a land plant as the roots are required to be almost constantly in contact with salty water and the leaves may be submerged twice daily in a salty water bath. Even if a land plant were able to withstand one or the other of these traumatic occurrences, the combination of the two would certainly be its ruin.

Out of the thousands of species of land plants in North America, only two species of grass, *Spartina alterniflora* and *Spartina patens,* thrive on this rigorous salty regime and dominate the marshes of the East Coast. They rule the marsh through sheer tonnage produced and space occupied. The rest of the marsh plants are like so many relatives attached to a strong household, of some importance in the social setup but of none in the chain of command.

The generic name *Spartina* comes from the Greek word for a cord which was made from a tough-leafed *Mediterranean Spartina*.

S. alterniflora is a big, coarse grass, with leaves which may be one half inch wide at the base and ten feet tall. A dense stand of this tall grass, growing in a spot where conditions are optimum for it, as along a tidal creek of our southeast coast, is like a small forest of dark green plants. Almost no light gets through to the mud beneath the stand. The wind is stilled among the stems and the humidity and temperature are high. Where it grows best, the tidal currents are moderately strong and most of the dead leaves are washed away. These forest-like stands are clean and free of debris most of the year.

Spartina patens is a fine, small grass, a complete contrast to *S. alterniflora*. Stands, which grow no taller than two feet, form an even carpet on the flats. Because the marsh flats are high and flooded only at the higher tides, and because they are protected from the currents by the *S. alterniflora* growing nearer the creeks, the dead growth of *S. patens* from the previous year is normally still present under the current growth. The ground is never exposed to the direct light, even in early spring, and remains moist year round. Numbers of animals depend on this protective mat of old grass for survival. Part the grass and you can discover them, living their busy lives hidden from view.

The current growth helps to form this protective mat as well as the previous year's crops. The stems are so fine that they are easily bent. But not only are they fine, they also have a weak area at their base so that they have a built-in tendency to bend. When one bends, it helps to bend its neighbor and the whole mass is finally forced quite flat but in a swirled pattern like a hair cowlick. In fact, these mats are called cowlicks. The built-in tendency to form cowlicks leads us to believe that the mats have a value for the plants as well as for the animals that live under them. Perhaps keeping the ground moist benefits *S. patens*.

Spartima patens grows best in large areas of level high marsh and also along the rows of flotsam at high tide mark. You can see the plants sticking up through a bed of drying eelgrass, each slender stalk topped in late summer by a number of one-sided purplish-red seed heads.

We will consider other marsh plants in detail in the next chapter, but since *Spartina's* existence in the wet-

Tall coarse Spartina alterniflora *growing along edges of a creek*

lands is such a dramatic success story, it takes first consideration.

There are many challenges to plants living in the marsh, lack of oxygen in the soil for instance, but since the presence of salt is such a traumatic addition to the diet of most plants, we will deal with this problem first and see why *Spartina* is able to adjust to even large concentrations of salt in water.

The cells of living organisms must be wet to function. All of the life processes occur in water solutions or mixtures. The exchange of essential materials with the environment takes place through wet membranes, such as breathing in lungs and absorption of food in intestines. But it is not enough that the living cells be wet. The concentration of water relative to the concentration of dissolved and suspended materials must be controlled within narrow limits or the system gets out of balance and the cells die.

When there is a different concentration of dissolved substances in the water on two sides of a wet membrane, water tends to move through the membrane. It moves from the less to the more concentrated solution, tending to make the concentrations equal. This movement is called osmosis. The concentration of salts within most higher plant cells is below that of seawater. When these cells are immersed in seawater, the water within the cells moves out through the cell walls by osmosis until the cell contents have the same concentration as the seawater. This loss of water kills the cell.

Spartina cells have adapted to this danger of water loss by increasing the concentration of salt in their internal water so that it is above the concentration of the seawater which surrounds them. Water moves into *Spartina* cells of other plants from freshwater.

Water tends to move into the plant cells by osmosis, but the cells have room for very little water. While water cannot move in once the cell is full, the tendency to move remains and exerts a pressure known as osmotic pressure. The pressure blows the cells up within their tough cellulose walls, in much the same way that an inner tube is blown up within a tire casing. Like the tire, the cell is stiffened by this internal pressure, giving the plant a good deal of its strength. The plant develops a "flat tire," it wilts, when it has lost either enough water or enough osmotic pressure so that the cells are no longer blown up within their walls.

The concentration of salts within the *Spartina* cells is kept above that of the water, not by increasing the concentration of all the salts in seawater, but by selecting those which have relatively little to do in the internal functioning of the cell, so that they will not upset the functions of the cell if they are concentrated.

The most common salt in the sea is sodium chloride, table salt, and it is that that the plants living in the salt marshes concentrate.

Sodium has little work to do in plants. It seems to be necessary for their growth, but even distilled water ordinarily contains enough sodium from contamination by dust to satisfy this need. Animals need much more sodium for their bodies. To meet their need, they have developed a taste for salt so that they go out looking for salty substances when they are salt hungry.

Salt marsh plants selectively absorb sodium from the water. Chloride comes with it to maintain electrical neutrality, and they continue to absorb sodium chloride until the internal concentration is high enough to prevent wilting. Along with the sodium, the plants usually concentrate potassium. But potassium seems to be important to their metabolism and must be more carefully controlled. At least it is usually concentrated to a lesser degree than is sodium.

The concentration of salt within the cells solves one problem connected with water balance, but there is another which must be solved by other techniques. *Spartina*, as well as the other higher plants on the marsh, gets its carbon dioxide, necessary for photosynthesizing food, from the air. Since exchanges between plants and their surroundings take place through wet membranes, the presence of a wet membrane in contact with the air inevitably leads to a loss of water from the membrane by evaporation.

Land plants have developed a fancy apparatus to keep this evaporation to a minimum and keep their needs for water down. They have restricted the wet surface to cavities within the leaves connected to the air by means of small holes, called stomata, in the otherwise waterproof leaf surface. These holes are numerous enough so that exchange between the air and the leaf is nearly as fast as it would be if the entire leaf surface

Windrow of Spartina *patens*

were a wet membrane. The holes, however, can be closed by special guard cells around the openings. When they are partly or completely closed, the evaporation from the leaf is very much reduced.

When the stomata are closed, water loss is prevented but so is the uptake of carbon dioxide, necessary for manufacturing food. The stomata are normally open most of the day while photosynthesis is taking place and closed when the plants are not photosynthesizing at night or when the leaves are full of sugar after having been functioning actively for some hours in good light. The closure of the stomata, when the plant is inactive, saves a significant amount of water.

Spartina, like the land plants from which it evolved, relies heavily on the stomata of its leaves for controlling evaporation. But then enters the complication of salt. For a plant like *Spartina*, getting its water from the sea, for every one hundred parts of water evaporated from the leaf surface, there are three parts of salt left behind somewhere. Most of this salt presents no disposal problem to the inner workings of the plant because it never goes into the plant at all.

Water is pulled into the plant through a membrane on the roots which excludes most of the salt. This salt remaining in the soil is then leached out by the water draining the marshes at low tide.

This pulling of water from the soil into the roots of plants is the device by which all higher land plants get water up into their leaves to replace that which evaporates. Or more correctly, the evaporating water pulls more water up after itself.

Water, for its deceptively weak appearance, is amazingly strong stuff. A thin, clean column will theoretically stand up to a pull of about ten thousand atmospheres or one hundred fifty thousand pounds per square inch, before breaking, making water stronger than steel. Strengths of two hundred atmospheres have been measured by spinning a fine tube of water about its center faster and faster until the water column breaks at the center. A thick column of water breaks easily because of cavitation, the formation of air bubbles pulled out of the water by the reduction of pressure. A gas has no strength but expands to fill any space available to it, and so, a gas bubble destroys all the strength of a water column. This tensile strength, or cohesion, is one of the important properties of water which determines the water balance within plants.

Another is the tendency of water, or any other fluid, to move from a region of higher pressure to one of lower. We are surrounded by examples of liquid water being pushed by pumps up through pipes and out into bathtubs and sinks when a valve is opened.

Water vapor obeys the same law. It moves from a place where the vapor pressure is higher to one where it is lower. Vapor pressures are usually referred to in terms of relative humidity, which is the extent to which the air is saturated with water vapor. Saturated air has a vapor pressure which is equal to that of liquid water at that temperature.

The air next to a water surface will be at the highest possible vapor pressure for that temperature, it will have a relative humidity of a hundred percent, and water vapor will move from it to drier air farther away which has a lower vapor pressure. As the air next to the water loses water vapor, water vapor will escape from the liquid water to replace it. This process is evaporation. The tendency of water to evaporate into air of any particular dryness can also be expressed in terms of pressure, as though dry air were pulling the water out of the liquid. A relative humidity of 98.2 percent pulls water out of liquid water with a force of about twenty-two atmospheres, three hundred thirty pounds per square inch.

Another important property of water which has to be considered in relation to higher plants is the osmotic pressure we have already referred to in *Spartina*. Osmotic pressure is the pressure with which a salt solution pulls water molecules from pure water, and is approximately proportional to the concentration of the solution.

The osmotic pressure of seawater is about twenty-five atmospheres. For contrast, the osmotic pressure of human blood is about eight atmospheres; the osmotic pressure of pure water is zero.

An example of the working of osmotic pressure in plants having freshwater at their roots can be seen in the Douglas fir. A Douglas fir tree reaching three hundred feet into the air is, like all plants, full of water. A water column, such as exists in the sapwood of that tree, needs a pressure of ten atmospheres to support it. The pressure can either be applied from the bottom as if by a pump, or it can be applied as a pull from the top. This pulling from the top that occurs in a plant has no analogy in mechanical devices. A lift pump, like an old-fashioned kitchen pitcher pump, depends on the push of air pressure to lift water and so cannot lift it more than thirty feet, the height to which fifteen pounds per square inch can push water.

Without concerning ourselves with the complicated

problem of how the water got into the tree in the first place, we will only worry about what happens once it is there. If the air is drier than about ninety-eight percent relative humidity, which it will be most of the time, the tendency of water to evaporate from the needles will be strong enough to pull a molecule into the sap at the roots for every one that leaves at the top. If the relative humidity is higher than ninety-eight percent, the pull of the column of water will be enough to keep the water from evaporating and will, theoretically, pull water into the plant from the air.

The sap is contained in special ducts within the plant, but all of the living cells are in contact with sap where it seeps through the porous cellulose structure of the stems and leaves. If the cells are to hold on to their water, they must have at least ten atmospheres of pull, and they need a bit more if they are to remain turgid or inflated and help support the plant. They develop the necessary pull by retaining salts and developing an osmotic pressure of a little more than ten atmospheres.

A short marsh plant existing in salt water is at the other extreme from the Douglas fir. The seawater around the plant has an osmotic pressure of twenty-five atmospheres. If water is to evaporate from the wet surface of the leaf, the air must pull it with the force of at least twenty-five atmospheres in order to pull it out of the seawater. The site of the separation of the salt from the water is on the surface of the roots of *Spartina* and red mangrove, in which the sap is almost completely fresh.

Sap from the roots up to the leaves is under tension, just as it is in the tall tree. In *Spartina*, the tension is greater than it is in the Douglas fir although the distance water must travel is much less. This is why all of the cells of *Spartina*, and not just the root cells in contact with the seawater, must concentrate salt within themselves in order to prevent wilting. Although the osmotic pressure of the water in contact with most of the cells is nearly zero, because the water inside the

conducting system, the sap, is nearly fresh, there is a
tension within this water produced by the pulling of
water molecules into the air against the osmotic pull of
seawater.

This process of pulling freshwater out of the sea
nearly solves the problem of *Spartina*, but for one thing.
The sap is nearly fresh but it still contains some salt.
The plant must get rid of this salt or it would accumulate, raise the osmotic pressure of the sap, and eventually kill the plant. Scattered over the surfaces of the
leaves of both *Spartina* and black mangrove, there are
special glands which can pick out the salt getting into
the sap through the root membranes. This gland secretes
the salt in very concentrated solution through special
pores that lead to the outside of the leaf. There the
water secreted with the salt usually evaporates and
leaves little salt crystals, which give off a minute sparkle
in the sun, until the next high tide washes them from
the leaves.

Spartina survives in the hostile atmosphere of the salt
marsh and endures the sea by keeping most of the salt
out of its sap, by secreting what little salt does get into
the sap, and by concentrating some of this same salt in
its cells so that they will be able to resist the tension
placed upon the sap by the evaporation occurring
through the stomata. It is a success story of the most
complicated nature.

The entire system has been constructed by natural
selection so that it functions with great economy. The
plant must have wet surfaces exposed to the air to get
the essential carbon dioxide from which it makes its
livelihood. The wet surface allows water to evaporate,
which must then be replaced if the plant is not to dry
up and die. So, the plant builds a set of small tubes
connecting the ground water with the leaves, closes the
tubes off at the lower end with a membrane which
allows water to pass but prevents the free passage of
salts, and fills the system with water. Except for getting
rid of the little excess salt which accumulates within the

system, the plant's work is finished and the system functions automatically.

Water evaporating from the moist membranes of the leaves pulls on the water in the tubes, which transmits the pull down to the membrane through which pure water is pulled from the seawater outside. Water cannot be pulled into the air unless it is pulled with enough force to pull water out of seawater. Each molecule lost by evaporation is automatically replaced. The system is in dynamic balance.

There is a great deal more to this story of the transport of water in plants. Much of it is poorly understood and there are many questions begging for an answer. Two of the most important questions are: how are the tubes filled in the first place; and what happens when there is an accidental break in the water column? For now, we will have to be content with what we know of the principal aspects of the water supply system of plants.

The pulling of water out of seawater requires energy which is supplied by the heat of the sun. The heat furnishes energy which evaporates the water and puts tension on the water columns in plants.

This heat falling on the leaves of the plant brings with it a problem. The heat must be disposed of before it raises the temperature of the leaf to a lethal level. As any swimmer knows, a brisk wind can evaporate the surface water from the body emerging from the water and cause an uncomfortable chill, or at least a cooling one. The temperature of leaves is partly kept within tolerable limits by this kind of evaporation.

All significant amounts of heat, as well as other forms of energy used by earthly organisms, come originally from the sun. The sun's energy is so common and abundant that, in spite of its prime importance, it is quite often overlooked as a source of anything but light.

Before anything else, first comes the sun, but the immediate sources of energy may be other than direct radiation from the sun, or sunshine. All things, warmer than absolute zero, radiate heat. Animals radiate heat from their bodies to the surroundings and the surroundings radiate back. The balance of radiation depends on the relative temperature between a body and the surroundings. You can tell if a radiator is hot without touching it, because the radiant heat from it that strikes your hand is greater than the heat your hand is radiating back. A cold pane of glass in the window will feel cold before you touch it for just the opposite reason, your hand loses more heat to it by radiation than it gets back.

Heat may also be gained by conduction. If two objects are in contact, heat will flow from the warmer to the cooler. Air is the substance to which we lose most heat by conduction. Air cannot carry much heat in comparison with other substances. Water, for example, can carry five times as much heat as an equal weight of air or nearly seven thousand times as much as an equal volume of air. The air is so fluid that, as soon as it gains a little heat and gets a little lighter, it moves up and away from the surface that warmed it. This allows cooler air to move in and bring the transfer of heat to a maximum. The process which can occur in fluids is called convection to distinguish it from ordinary conduction to a nonfluid substance.

A *Spartina* leaf growing on the salt marsh on an ordinary summer day with a clear sky gets about twenty-one percent of its heat directly from the sun, four percent by reflection of sunlight from the ground, surroundings and sky, thirty-four percent by radiation from the air, and forty-one percent by radiation from the ground and surroundings, mostly other *Spartina* leaves. All the heat is gained by radiation. On a hot day there is no gain by convection from the air, since the leaves are usually warmer than the air.

Since the leaves do not get hotter and hotter, the heat must be leaving the leaves as fast as it is coming in. It is lost by radiation from the leaf back to its surroundings, by convection and by evaporation. Most of the radiation is heat that is bounced back and forth between the leaves. The net gain of heat is from the object warmer than the leaves, the sun. The net loss by radiation is to the object that is colder than the leaves, which is the sky. It is for the same reason that it is more comfortable to be exposed to the sun but protected from exposure to the northern sky on a cold day. The opposite is true on a hot day in summer.

It is possible to calculate that, even if there was no evaporation from the leaves, they would have to be only ten to fifteen degrees warmer than the air in order to lose heat as fast as they gain it. Since they are constantly losing water, they are actually only a few degrees warmer than the air.

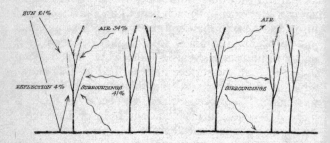

Heat gains and losses in Spartina

This is not the case for the larger leaves of plants, such as trees, which do not lose heat as readily by convection as do the long, thin grass leaves. The leaf of an oak tree that wasn't evaporating water would get to be about forty degrees warmer than the air before its temperature ceased to rise. On a bright summer day, that would be hot enough to kill the leaf. Unlike some other plants, *Spartina* could survive even the hottest weather without any water loss if water loss were connected only with temperature maintenance.

The muds of salt marshes are almost uniformly devoid of oxygen. Because they are flooded by the tides frequently, the air spaces in the soil are filled with water through which gases, such as oxygen, move extremely slowly. At the same time, since the surface of the marsh soil is a very active area with many bacteria and higher organisms living there in great numbers, the oxygen consumption at the soil surface is very high. It is so high that, even though some oxygen is carried into the soil with the water that percolates down each time the tide falls, the oxygen supply is reduced to zero below the top few tenths of an inch.

Spartina roots, like most living things, require oxygen for their life processes. They suffocate if deprived of oxygen. Since the bacteria and other organisms in the top layers of mud have usurped most of the available oxygen, the plants are left with a real problem. *Spartina* has solved this problem in its usual efficient way, by evolving a neat system which functions according to physical laws without further effort after the initial construction.

A set of hollow tubes runs from the leaves down into hollow spaces within the roots. All of these spaces are filled with air and are open to the air through the stomata on the leaves. This provides oxygen by a direct pipeline from the air, in through the stomata, down the leaves, through the stems and rhizomes, and into the roots. The mechanism by which it travels is called diffusion, the process by which a substance moves molecule by molecule from a region where it is more concentrated to a region where it is less concentrated. Diffusion occurs in all states of matter: gases, liquids, and solids. It operates fastest in gases because the molecules are much freer to move in relation to each other than they are in other states. It is not necessary that there by any flow of the medium containing the diffusing substance. The diffusing molecules move between the other molecules in the medium. In other words, it is not necessary for the air in the *Spartina* air ducts to move in toward

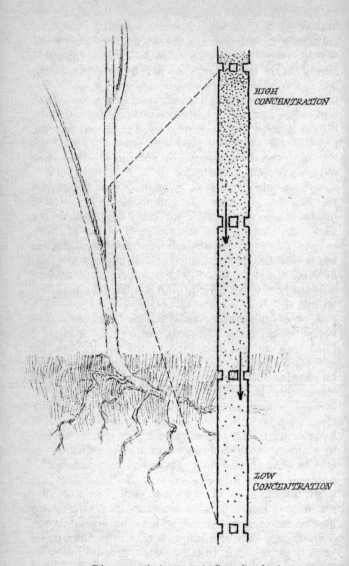

Diagram of air space in Spartina *leaf*

the roots in order for the oxygen to diffuse from the air to the roots.

Oxygen is consumed by the *Spartina* roots so that the oxygen concentration there is low and carbon dioxide is given off. The concentration of this product of respiration is high. In the air outside, oxygen is high and carbon dioxide low. Diffusion moves more oxygen in and carbon dioxide out. All the plant has to do to make this system function properly is to construct the air passages of sufficient diameter to allow enough room for the necessary amounts of diffusion to take place.

Diffusion is only one ten-thousandth as fast in water as it is in air, so the passage must not be allowed to fill with water at high tide when there is danger of flooding the air passages. *Spartina* simply closes the stomata on the leaf surfaces. The passages remain dry.

Actually, the gas spaces in the roots of *Spartina* are larger than necessary for the diffusion of enough oxygen to keep the roots alive. There is excess oxygen which is supplied to the mud just around the roots by diffusion through the walls of the roots. If you dig a *Spartina* plant out of the mud you will see that around the larger roots, the mud has changed from its normal gray or black color to a reddish-brown. This is a result of a change of iron in the mud from the reduced form of iron sulfide, in which it exists in the oxygen-free mud, to the more familiar form of iron oxide, or rust. Although the matter has not been studied to our knowledge, there may well be a number of tiny animals, such as nematodes, which take advantage of this and make their home in the oxygenated layer within the oxygen-free mud.

It has been suggested that the air-filled roots of plants such as *Spartina* serve as anchors for the plant in soft mud. Since these are also the plants most exposed to strong tidal currents, they need a solid anchorage system. Perhaps the air-filled center of the roots enables them to construct an increased root surface for holding on to the mud without using a corresponding increase

Diagram of an open and closed leaf stoma

in plant material for new construction. This is a good example of the economy of nature in using air for a building material, as well as a transport mechanism for necessary oxygen.

In spite of its adaptation to the salt marsh, living there costs *Spartina* something extra in getting rid of excess salt, in not being able to function at all times of day, and in having its activity restricted to periods of low tide. In fact, when the plants are artificially grown, they do best in freshwater. It seems strange that these plants are common only in salt marshes. This, again, is because of *Spartina*'s unique physiology.

Spartina plants have an unusually high requirement for iron, one of the essential nutrients for plant growth. In the marsh mud, iron is trapped by forming iron sulfide with the abundant sulfide present there. Any dissolved iron, carried by the tidal waters that percolate down into the mud with each fall in tide, is left behind in the mud. The trapped iron is insoluble in water, so it cannot be carried away. For the same reason, it is unavailable to a plant which can absorb metals only from solution in the water around their roots. But wherever in the mud the roots of *Spartina* go, they carry with them a supply of oxygen which oxidizes the iron sulfide, forming as one product the highly soluble iron, ferrous sulfate, which can be picked up by *Spartina*. This supplies the plant with the abundant iron which it needs. The plant can grow in areas which have less available iron, but it does not do well.

Wherever a plant does less than well, there are other plants that can do better. The better adapted plants grow faster, taller, and thicker, while the more poorly adapted do just the opposite. They are crowded out often before they are even recognizable.

Most plants cannot live on the salt marsh. The *Spartinas* have inherited these bits of earth and reign there by default from lack of competition, and by their efforts in overcoming the hazards of this difficult habitat.

8. Other Marsh and Border Plants

ALTHOUGH "SPARTINA" RULES, OTHER PLANTS HAVE adapted, more or less successfully, to the rigorous conditions of marsh living. Few of them have common names, as common names develop only when a plant is of enough interest to be singled out by a number of people. There is scant pedestrian traffic over the marsh, so few plants have been singled out. When they have and have been given a common name, it might be quite local. The same plant may carry another common name in another area.

Some common names are too general to be useful, such as "marsh grass," "salt hay," or "salt grass," which apply to everything grasslike growing on the marsh. Other common names are not common names at all but translations of the Latin or Greek scientific names. Usually we will write of these plants formally, using their proper titles. As well as *Spartina*, some other names will occur repeatedly: *Distichlis, Juncus,* mangrove, and *Salicornia*.

Distichlis spicata, a short, fine grass, shares the higher marsh levels with its look-alike sister, *Spartina paten.* In some areas it may grow in a fairly pure stand. *D. spicata* seems to be better able to withstand the more waterlogged spots of high marsh and may predominate in such areas.

There are a number of ways in which the two grasses can be distinguished. The seeds of *distichlis* protrude on both sides of rather short heads and give a prickly

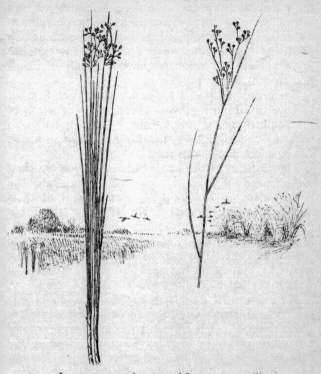

Juncus roemerianus *and* Juncus gerardii

appearance to the fruiting area. The seeds are white rather than colored. The leaves are conspicuously arranged along opposite sides of the stem instead of coming from the base without a special arrangement as they seem to do in *Spartina.* The leaves of *S. patens* are rolled on the edges, more than those of *Distichlis.* The two can even be distinguished from a distance in winter, for the *S. patens* areas with their tightly rolled leaves and thinner stems appear grayer than areas of the more straw-colored *Distichlis.*

Rushes often form a border on the landward side of

the grassy marshes and even form extensive marshes themselves in certain places where there is some freshwater entering the salt marshes. *Juncus gerardii* in the north and *Juncus roemerianus* in the south are grasslike in appearance but belong to another family of plants that grow in marshy places.

These two salt marsh rushes are quite dark in color and are called black grass or black rush. The leaves of the southern species are tubular instead of flat, with wickedly pointed tips. A walk through a *Juncus* marsh can be a torture of stab wounds.

The marshes to the north of the *Spartina* marshes, those in arctic Canada, are covered with grasses. The principal species is *Puccinellia phryganodes,* which is replaced by *P. maritima* a bit farther south. These grasses are shorter than southern marsh *Spartina alterniflora* and rather coarse compared to the fine *Spartina patens*. Still, the arctic marshes, during their short summer, take on the neat, managed look that is characteristic of the salt marshes along coastal United States.

A new view of the marsh appears in south Florida where the *Spartina* flats begin to be replaced by mangrove swamps. Wherever mangrove can live, they crowd out other plants by growing taller and shading the shorter species dependent on direct sunlight for survival. If they do not actually replace all other species, they dominate the landscape anyway, because of their size.

There are two species, the black mangrove, *Avicennia nitida*, and the red, *Rhizophora mangle*. Both are shrubby plants at the northern limit of their range but grow to be seventy or eighty feet tall from southern Florida to the tropics. In the more accessible parts of Florida, mangroves are about twenty feet tall with trunks four to eight inches in diameter.

Both species have remarkable root structures which are visible above ground. The red mangrove puts out prop roots from the stem which arch down into the mud, often giving off other arching roots on the way.

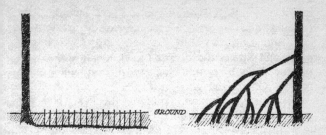

Diagram of black and red mangrove roots

Roots also grow down from the lower branches of the trees, into the mud, and finally become stems themselves with their own prop roots. The underground roots of the black mangrove grow horizontally. At intervals they send up branches that reach into the air like fingers. The result of either kind of root growth is an impenetrable tangle.

In other parts of the world, salt marshes may be occupied by a greater variety of plants, differing in abundance to be sure, but all common enough that the marshes have a varied look. North of southern Florida, on our East Coast, the plant cover of the salt marshes is so uniform that it resembles planted crops more than a natural mixed vegetation.

There are many other seed plants on the marshes than the ones we have mentioned, but these are relatively rare and do not lend much to the characteristic look of the marsh. They occur, mostly, at the landward edge of the marsh and are more characteristic of the border, the intermediate zone between marsh and dry land, than they are of the marsh. These are plants that can withstand salt rather than plants which are well adapted to living in salty soils or plants which prefer salty soils.

Well up on land, past the intermediate zone, there are plants which live near seashores because they can tolerate being bathed with salt spray during storms, but cannot endure salt at their roots. These include plants recommended for seaside gardens like the Eastern red cedar and American holly. Bayberry grows well in such places and makes the border of the marsh a collecting spot for "colonial candle" makers who copy their ancestors by melting the gray-green waxy coating from the berries in a pot of water, skimming the wax which rises to the top, and then dipping the fragrant candles. Myrtle warblers, which survive on these berries during the winter, compete with candle makers for the crop. The leaves are also dried and used for soup flavoring, in the manner of the tropical bay leaves which you buy in the store.

Other resistant plants are less friendly and productive. Poison ivy survives all storms, and grows vigorously on marsh borders from New England to Florida. It is often found in such large stands that it closes an area to all foot traffic.

Since salt marshes are occupied mainly by grasses, which have insignificant flowers, there are few blossoms of any size to be seen. Most of the large flowers that do bloom are found in the border plants. In the summer, the rose mallow displays large hollyhock-like flowers, all pink or cream colored with a red center. This plant is the source of the large flowered mallows grown in flower gardens, but the species is most beautiful when unexpectedly sighted at the edge of the sea.

Later in the year, there are the yellows of the seaside goldenrod, a fleshy leaved plant which has the flowers balanced above the stem rather than suspended from one side. From Virginia south, the sea oxeye, a low shrub with yellow sunflower-like blossoms, can be found. Purple thistle and sea pinks are able to grow in areas of low salt concentration.

Iva best characterizes the border between marsh and land. This shrubby growth with thickish leaves is quite uninteresting and bears greenish flowers. It resembles a close relative, the ragweed, but does not produce a rash of sneezes. Another name for *Iva* is marsh elder. It has

Seaside goldenrod

little to recommend it as a decorative plant but is abun
dant in border marsh, growing in thickets of from two
to twelve feet tall. It even grows out on the marsh itself
in spots where the ground level is high, caused by a
natural island, the remains of an old dike, on the spoils
from dredging operations, or on the material dug out in
making mosquito ditches.

On the higher parts of the marsh near the border,
two flowers are found in some numbers, sea lavender
and salt marsh aster. They have attracted enough attention to be recommended in books on wildflower garden-
ing, but can be grown only at seacoast homes. The
leaves of the sea lavender grow close to the ground in a
rosette. In late summer a stalk of flowers like a tiny
cloud of lavender mist appears. These flowers are

Marsh elder

strawlike and are gathered for winter bouquets. The aster, with purple to white flowers, is attractive but skimpy. It suffers by comparison with the many other asters blooming over the countryside and is not as showy as the lavender.

In the gentian family, noted for its bright blossoms, are two lovely flowers that have adapted to living with their roots in salty soil. Both are called sea pinks, *Sabatia stellaris* with five petals, and the larger *S. dodecandra* with ten to twelve petals. Both have pink flowers with yellow centers that add a gay touch in the late summer to marshes which have them nestled in the grass. These might well be tried in gardens for they are as attractive as many common garden flowers.

Gerardia maritima sometimes puts on quite a blossom show on the upper parts of the marshes. The flowers have rose-colored petals at the end of a red-spotted pink bell. They grow atop wiry stems with narrow, slightly fleshy leaves. Very similar *Gerardias* grow in bogs, fields, and forests but none stand out like those blooming against the green background of salt marsh.

Several species of *Salicornia* live on the salt marsh proper. They can best be divided into the perennial and annual types. Both are shrubby, swollen little green plants projecting up from the sand which they prefer as home. The common names for this group are different in various geographical areas. To some people they are chicken toe, because of their shape, saltwort to others, because of their salty taste, and glasswort to still others, because of the slightly translucent look due to the plant being full of water.

They are also known as pickle plant and marsh samphire, this latter name coming from their resemblance to a European fleshy seaside plant known as the herb of St. Peter. In English it became samphire from the French, St. Pierre.

The perennial species of *Salicornia* has a woody center in the stems. The annual varieties are soft throughout and the young plants were formerly used to give a salty tang to salads. The plant has been used as a pickle for a long time, substituted for the true samphire of Europe by the colonists who lived along the marsh. These pickles were so well liked that it was suggested by some colonists that those not fortunate enough to live along the marshes should cultivate samphire in their kitchen gardens. We have made them, following a recipe given by Euell Gibbons in *Stalking the Blue-Eyed Scallop*, and found the samphire pickles delicious.

The annual species, like the European samphire, turn bright red in the fall. Bits of marsh with *Salicornia* take on a very festive appearance with some bright red plants, some still green, and every hue between.

There are some other rather inconspicuous, but interesting plants on the salt marshes and sandy shores.

Sea lavender

Several species of the genus *Atriplex* occur. They are
hard to distinguish and all are called orache, a corruption of the Latin name, or spearscale in reference to the
shape of the leaves. Another group is in the genus
Suaeda, called sea blite, which is again a corruption of
the Latin name. These plants are highly variable in
shape, from upright shrubby to prostrate, insignificant-
looking plants. *Atriplex* have thick spear- or arrow-

shaped leaves while those of *Suaeda* are narrow and swollen. *Salsola kali,* which is also called saltwort, is very similar to *Suaeda* except that the tips of its leaves are armed with a spine. This plant is a variety of the Russian thistle, a troublesome weed, named because of its spines and place of origin. None of these plants has a flower worth consideration. All, along with *Salicornia,* are members of the goosefoot family, the *Chenopodiaceae.*

Many members of the *Chenopodiaceae* are weeds such as the pigweeds and lamb's quarters. Beets, swiss chard, and spinach are also members of this family which have been enlarged in usefulness by man. All of the marsh members are edible, as are the weeds just mentioned, and are rather good as either raw or cooked greens. The fact that these plants had common names in Greek and Latin may well indicate that they were eaten commonly at one time, and have only fairly recently slipped off the table.

There is another set of plants on the marsh, even less conspicuous, the microscopic algae. Diatoms, within their tiny silica pillbox skeletons, may cover the surface of the mud. Tiny green flagellates occur with them. Both of these are so small that they can be seen only as a coloring of the mud, a golden or greenish hue.

Blue-green algae also live on the marsh. Some are filamentous and occur in large enough colonies to be visible. The blue-green algae are tough for their size. Some manage to grow throughout the year even as far north as Massachusetts, though others appear only in the summer. They form dark blue-green sheets, ribbons and mounds on the creek banks, as well as under the *Spartina* growth. They even occur in the dim light under the dense growth of the *S. patens* marshes. The blue-green algae are very primitive plants which lack organized nuclei in their cells.

There are also a few photosynthetic bacteria, the most primitive of all plants, on the marsh. The most noticeable are the purple sulfur bacteria. These minute

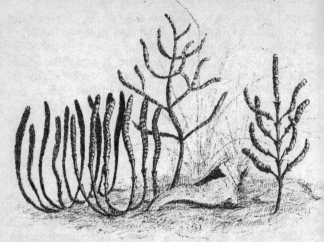

Salicornia virginica, *perennial; and* S. europaga *and*
S. bigelovii, *annual species*

plants sometimes color wide swaths of sand, laid bare at
low tide, and can usually also be found just under the
surface of the mud around ribbed mussels growing on
the marsh. They are peculiar in that they cannot stand
to live where there is any oxygen, but since they are
photosynthetic, they must be in the light like any green
plant. They are limited to the layer of mud or sand just
below the surface where the oxygen from the air is
already used up but where light can still penetrate. On
the sandy bottom of a marsh creek at low tide you can
often uncover an intense purple color by scraping off
just the slightest layer of surface sand. Occasionally the
intense color is accidentally exposed by water currents
but the bacteria so exposed to oxygen in the air die.

Although there are, perhaps, many millions of times
more bacteria and algae on the marsh than grasses, the
grasses are the plants that are first noticed when you
look at the marsh. The grasses that grow there successfully look like grasses. There is nothing about their

Suaeda maritima *and* Atriplex

pattern of growth or the form of the plant that you
notice as being different from other grasses. Contrast
that with the mangroves, which immediately attract attention because of their peculiar roots. Since there is no
easily visible modification of the grasses to the salt
marsh habitat, you must consider how just being a grass
helps *Spartina* live in this peculiar environment.

Grasses are either annual or perennial. The perennials are bunch or creeping grasses. *Spartina* belongs to
the latter group. The underground part of the plant is
perennial, that is, it lives from year to year. The top is
annual and dies each fall. This is a variation of the
typical situation found in temperate-zone perennials.
One part of the plant lives a long time, whether root or
root and stem, and one part dies each year, the leaves,

and perhaps the stem as well. *Spartina* keeps its underground stem, the rhizome, as well as its roots alive and only the aerial stem dies each autumn.

In a bunch grass, the protected part of the stem divides but doesn't grow laterally. In a creeping grass, some stem buds, instead of growing directly up into the air, grow laterally first and cause the grass to spread from its original position in the soil.

During most of its life, the *Spartina* stem is underground. Only the leaves extend into the air. But when the flowering time approaches, the whole stalk begins to lengthen. The area between the nodes of the stalk, marked by walls across the hollow stem from which each leaf grows, stretches out. The leaves, which rose from the ground level in the spring, now rise from a visible stalk in the air. Finally the bud gives rise to the flower, a rather insignificant one as is usual with grasses, and with this flowering, the plant is finished. New buds form on the underground part of the stem for next year's visible plants.

The success of grasses in general, and *Spartina* in the salt marsh in particular, depends in large part on the manner of growth. Having a part of the stem growing underground provides obvious protection from the winter cold. The stem is also protected from fires which are quite common to grasslands. Marshes are by no means excluded from having fires just because the soil is wet. We have seen several marsh fires burn for days with large billows of white smoke rising from small visible flames.

In the case of either fire or freezing, the leaves and stalk of one year's growth are destroyed, but the perennial part of the grass, the underground stem or rhizome with its bud and roots, survives to grow another year.

On the salt marsh, this growth habit provides protection from ice as well. On many freshwater marshes, ice may form and melt without doing much damage to the plants growing there, because there is little movement of the ice. On a salt marsh, the ice which forms must move up and down with the tides, and on any extensive marsh tides exist or the marsh would not exist. Since the salt marsh always has connections with the sea, there is a good chance that a winter storm will push water and ice across the surface. The ice will plane off everything projecting above the mud and dig in only slightly, especially if the mud surface is frozen. The stem and buds are left intact and in place beneath the surface, waiting for the spring thaws.

One reason that no tree has adapted to life on a northern marsh, as mangrove has to the south, is that a tree could not survive where wind- and tide-driven blocks of ice would cut off newly established seedlings. To survive a northern winter on the marshes, plants must hide under frozen mud.

In late summer, however, the grass which has done well by keeping everything but the leaves down in the mud, suddenly sends up a slender flower stalk which waves about in the wind in a manner characteristic of all grasses. This exposure is necessary because all grasses are wind pollinated.

Grass flowers are not usually thought of as flowers, a distinction shared with other wind-pollinated flowers, such as pinecones. Neither grass flowers nor pinecones need showy petals or sweet scents to attract the capricious breezes. They just need to make themselves available, which the grasses do by thrusting the flower stalks above the leaves where they can give their pollen to the slightest wind movement.

Pollen chambers grow on threadlike stems reaching out into the air where the pollen may easily escape, giving the early flower stalk a furry look. Even a gentle breeze will set grass flowers moving. The flower stalks sway and the pollen chambers tremble. Microscopic pollen grains escape into the air where they blanket an area with an invisible cloud. The purpose of all this is

Grass flowers standing above leaves

to get a supply of pollen to each plant, as at least one pollen grain must arrive for each seed that is to develop.

Most animals are of only one sex. This provides no chance for self-fertilization, the ultimate in inbreeding. But most higher plants have both sexes on one plant, even in each flower, and yet, to maintain vigor within the species, it is to their advantage to have crossbreeding. Various plants have different ways of achieving cross-fertilization, many are concerned with the habits of insects that pollinate them. Grasses, being wind pollinated, protrude their pollen sacs and shed their pollen before the female part of the same flower has had time to develop to the point where it can be fertilized. The chance of pollen being carried on the winds and returned to fertilize the flower from which it came is extremely slight.

The wind does not select the spot where the pollen is to be deposited, as do insects, which go directly from plant to plant. Most of wind-distributed pollen is wasted by blowing onto other, unlike plants, or dumped onto the ground, or in the water.

Usually, pollen will not fertilize an alien flower, but occasionally it happens in closely related species and a new plant, a hybrid, is suddenly born. This rare event happened to *Spartina* sometime in the last century, *Spartina alterniflora* from North America appeared in England in the early part of the nineteenth century. Subsequently, it hybridized with *Spartina maritima* to give rise to *Spartina townsendii,* which has been very successful in colonizing mud flats on both sides of the English Channel.

Since most new *Spartina* plants are started by rhizomes, the seeds produced are important for only the occasional task of starting growth on a newly exposed sand or mud bank. Occasionally a new bit of marsh is created on such a spot by a bit of living rhizome which has been torn away from the parent plant by water currents or ice and dropped at a new site. One can come across these tough, underground stems, with roots extending from each node, cast up on the edges of marsh creeks.

Starting a marsh from seed is a chancy business. Seeds often require special conditions before they will germinate, and after they germinate, the tender seedlings are less tolerant of adverse growing conditions than are the adults.

As we have said before, the seeds of many marsh plants will not germinate in water which has the salt content of seawater, that is, water containing three and one half percent salt. Many salt marshes flourish in areas, such as river mouths, where the salinity is a happy mixing of sea and freshwater. Here, seeds have little trouble getting started. In other marshes, where full-strength seawater floods the ground, many seeds must wait until spring rains sweeten the soil sufficiently for them to germinate.

Salicornia seeds are the exception. They will germinate in water that is even saltier than seawater. They can colonize extreme spots like the tops of sandbanks above normal high tides where the water has been concentrated by evaporation until its salt content may be several times that of the sea.

Mangrove, again, shows a different pattern of seeding. The seeds germinate before they fall from the parent plant. The seeds of the red mangrove even put their first root out while they are still within the fruit hanging down from a branch. As the root grows, often to as long as twelve inches, it develops an enlarged tip at the end. Since this enlarged tip is the heaviest part of the seed, it is an effective device for driving the root into the mud when the seed falls from the parent plant. If

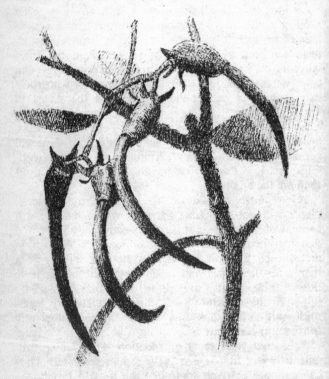

Red mangrove seeds germinating on the tree

there is a high tide when the seedling is mature and breaks away, it falls into the water but does not spear itself into the mud. It dives into the water a distance, bobs back up to the surface, and floats away.

The mangrove seedling is very hardy and can live a long time floating about on the water. At first, it floats horizontally but gradually the root grows denser. After a month or so, any seedling still flowing free has moved to a vertical position. The root continues to grow heavier and finally pulls the entire plant underwater. This process may take a year to complete, with the seedling still in good condition.

If the water is brackish rather than full-strength seawater, the process is shortened and the seedling becomes vertical sooner and sinks sooner. This works out well for mangrove, because brackish water is found along the coast where the seedling must lodge if it is to survive. And if it chances to lodge in mud which is no more than two feet underwater or mud that is exposed at low tide, the mangrove seedling may thrive and the mangrove forest spread.

A few marsh plants are annuals, depending on seeds not only to colonize new areas but to survive from one year to the next in areas that have already been colonized. These include the annual *Salicornia,* some *Suaeda*, the *Salsola* saltwort, and the attractive *Gerardia*. The adult annual plant dies after setting its seeds, and if the seeds fail to germinate and grow, the species disappears from the marsh. The advantage in depending on seeds to propagate each year is that no part of the parent plant needs to survive the winter. The embryonic plant within the seed is protected from physical damage by the storage tissue around it and the seed coat over it.

It is protected from a certain degree of cold by its dryness. Water expands when frozen and takes up more space than it does as a liquid. The disruption of cells by the expansion of water as it forms ice crystals is one of the principal dangers to freezing tissue. If there is little water in the cells, the disruption due to freezing will be correspondingly slight.

Much of the water in seeds has the safeguard of being "bound," joined to other molecules in such a way that it does not easily disengage itself to join with other water molecules to form ice. The tough seed is an excellent device for wintering over.

When conditions become more favorable in the spring, when the sun begins to warm things again, the seeds absorb water and begin to grow. A disadvantage which seeds have becomes evident. The process of seed growth, bursting of the seed coat, putting the shoot up into the light and the root in the soil for nourishment, is a slow one. Unless the seed is unusually large, there is little stored food. The first leaves must get into the light to produce the substance from which it will make subsequent leaves, stem, and roots. By contrast, the perennial plant can get off to a good start with the first rays of the warm sun because it can use stored food to form its new leaves and it already has a root system. By the time the seedling has produced a few leaves and is ready to start really living, some hardy perennial may have achieved such strong growth that the seedling is shaded out. All the early flowers in our gardens are perennials or biennials that stored up energy the previous year. It is midsummer before the annuals begin to bloom.

Annuals are rarer in nature than one would think. In most areas, where conditions are not as severe as in the desert or where man or animals have not dug up the ground and destroyed the perennials, the annuals cover little ground. This is the situation in the salt marsh. Annuals are most commonly found on areas of new sandbank growing out of the sea, which have not yet been invaded by suitable perennials. They also cover disturbed areas such as paths where the perennials were killed by trampling.

Although seeds have a difficult time getting started, plants must produce seeds if they are to take advantage of new situations created by the ceaseless changes in nature: the death of old plants, washouts due to flooding, drying of the soil from long droughts.

But to the total picture of the marsh, seeds are of little importance. There are large areas of marsh where conditions are less than ideal for grasses, where seeds are produced only sporadically. Yet the grasses grow there year after year, slowly adding old leaves and roots to the mud and building the level of the marsh higher.

On the more productive parts of the marsh, the grass grows tall. Every stalk is topped with a heavy seed head, but most of these seeds will come to nothing as far as the grass is concerned. The seeds will be eaten by migrating birds; they will germinate under favorable conditions but fail to survive; they will fall on hostile soil. But one in a million, or a billion, will find a new untried spot and give rise to a new, abundant marsh.

9. Marsh Animals

ANIMALS OCCUPY THE ENTIRE EXTENT OF THE MARSH. The tidal flats and marsh creek banks, exposed to the air less than half the time, are the estuarine habitat closest in space and environmental conditions to the marsh. (A slightly higher flat can be colonized by *Spartina* and becomes part of the marsh.) The inhabitants of these flats and banks are almost entirely animals which burrow in sand or mud, or both. Under the bare surface of the flat, the environment is relatively stable, sheltered from the extremes of variation. Razor clams, quahogs, clam worms, soft-shelled clams, lugworms, burrowing shrimp, and many more live there.

Other animals use the flats but do not live there. They are visitors at high tide or low, depending on whether they live in the air or in the water. Fish and crabs swim or walk in with the tides to eat any permanent inhabitants foolish enough to venture outside their burrows at the wrong moment. Shorebirds and a few insects come in on the wind to feed or rest on the open areas exposed by the fallen tide. Great numbers of gulls and terns can often be seen sitting, all facing one direction, between meals, as if contemplating the world together.

Conditions are relatively stable in the flat but changes occur and the animals living there must adapt to them. Organisms are mixtures of complex chemicals which can only react in the proper fashion to produce life, under fairly limited conditions. All organisms spend a great deal of their time and energy maintaining these conditions within themselves.

It is easier to maintain a relatively constant internal condition if the environment is not very variable. If the temperature changes only within narrow limits, there is no necessity to evolve a mechanism to deal with greater changes. The energy which would have to be used to cope with such changes can be used for some other purpose, perhaps more efficient feeding or better protection from predators. The same is true for the saltiness of the water supply to the organisms. If the water an animal encounters is always as salty as the sea, or is always as fresh as a lake or river, only the problems of dealing with that kind of water need be solved. If salinity changes irregularly, the animals' problem of adjustment is increased tremendously.

The possibilities for dealing with environmental changes are many. Mammals and birds cope with temperature changes by keeping their internal temperature constant over wide ranges of external temperature by producing extra heat when cold, and evaporating water and exposing themselves to cooling winds when hot. Some animals regulate their temperature by choosing spots with suitable temperatures, like coming out in the sun from the shade when they are cold and hiding in the shade when the sun is hot.

It is a general rule that, in environments with large variations in temperature, salinity, exposure, there are few species of animals to be found. Probably the difficulty of adapting to the great changes has limited the number of forms that have made the effort successfully.

For the estuarine animals in the tidal flats, many of the variations of their environment a few inches above them are smoothed out by their blanket of mud. Temperature changes are slower and less extreme one inch in the mud than at the surface and the same is true of changes in salinity. The water held in the interstices of the sediment moves only slowly and large, swift changes in water quality that occur at the surface penetrate slowly. If the water changes back to the original condition within a short time, the temporary change might not be apparent at all a short way down in the mud.

Estuarine animals, in general, have adapted to the changes of salinity and temperature characteristic of shallow inshore waters. The tide flat forms, though protected from fast changes, still must be able to resist the slower changes that occur from week to week throughout the year.

Most marine invertebrates are in osmotic equilibrium with seawater. Although the total concentration of internal salts equals that of the sea, the concentrations of the individual salts that make up the total are different. The animals must secrete the excess salts that diffuse into their bodies and they must collect from the water salts that are more concentrated in their bodies and are continually diffusing out.

Although they can deal with differences in concentrations of individual salts, they cannot deal with differences in total concentration. If the concentration of seawater surrounding them changes, their internal concentration changes. If their internal concentration changes by very much, they die. Such animals obviously cannot survive on the salt marsh.

There are some forms which, although their body fluids match the concentration of the water, are able to survive considerable changes in their internal salt concentration. The lugworm living in the flats is one of these. When rains freshen the water draining from the marsh, the lugworm's higher internal concentration draws water in and it swells up like a balloon. Then, more slowly than water enters, the salts leak out until a new balance is reached. The lugworm is again in osmotic balance with its surroundings. A change in the other direction shrivels the worm for a time before equilibrium is reached. Hiding in the sand helps keep the lugworm insulated from such osmotic insults to its body.

In addition to adjusting to temperature and salinity

changes, tide flat animals must be able to withstand the short periods of exposure which occur every time the tide goes out, if they are to live in the lower borders of the marsh. Since most live in permanent burrows in the mud, they can merely retreat into the deeper parts of their holes during low tides. But in so avoiding exposure, they encounter another serious problem. The salt marsh muds are completely without oxygen and will, in fact, rapidly take up oxygen out of any water with which they come in contact. When an animal digs a hole in the mud, the walls quickly consume the oxygen and oxygen in the water falls to zero. As long as there is water above the hole, the animal merely pumps more water in and keeps a supply of oxygen at hand. However, when the tide goes out, renewal of the water is impossible and the water cannot be reoxygenated from the air because too little is exposed at the entrance. Unless the hole drains completely and air enters, the oxygen supply will rapidly disappear. The animal must then be able to live without oxygen if it is to survive until the tide rises again. The animals manage this by slowing their activities and either possessing a high tolerance for, or excreting, the poisons produced during the wasteful anoxic metabolism.

Once the marsh occupies a flat, the openness is gone. Plants, which cover the space that was open country, provide a protective haven, new places to live above the mud and new sources of food. They slow the wind and moderate the weather, which opens the area for new animals.

Many of the animals that live on the flats continue their residence after *Spartina* gets started, but many move out when roots and rhizomes make burrowing in the mud difficult.

Near low water level, as near to the sea as it is possible to be and yet still be part of the marsh, tiny flower-like animals, hydroids, grow in clusters. Sea squirts and barnacles fasten themselves to any suitable solid surface in the same area. They are not really true marsh inhabitants but are sea creatures that as larvae search for a solid substratum as a foundation for home. They will settle on *Spartina* leaves and stems at high tide as well as stones or shells projecting from the mud along the creek banks. They seldom get far into the marsh but stop at the first solid surface they encounter.

Settling on the first solid surface encountered has its dangers. The soft-bodied forms that have, by chance, lodged on too high a spot are killed when later exposed during sunny low tides. Most hydroids, anemones, and tunicates can withstand only minor variations in salinity. They have no means of protecting themselves from the deadly effects of drying and heat. Even a short exposure to the summer midday sun can leave them a little withered bundle of nothing.

Barnacles, with their closable, shells, can withstand the sun's rays. They can shut out rain and freshwater runoff that might dilute them to death. They often live high in the tide zone on pilings found along the marsh creeks, but the flexibility of *Spartina* leaves is a barnacle's undoing in the marsh. Those that settle on the upper parts of the plants fall off when the leaf bends and destroys the barnacles's firm hold on its support, so necessary for its sessile way of life. They are found only near the base of the leaves, and even there, not in great numbers.

Though these animals live above ground, they often have an oxygen problem similar to the hole dwellers. Since they have no waterproof skin, they must close themselves up as much as possible to prevent drying. Anemones withdraw their tentacles and barnacles and mollusks close their shells. But the tighter they are closed, the less they can breathe and so they must also live without oxygen if they are to survive the low tide period.

The aboveground dwellers have another problem. They are exposed to weather. A hot sun at low tide in the summer or a freezing period at winter low tide can kill many that cannot stand the added temperature

Marsh edge with barnacles and mussels

stress. It is not surprising that the estuarine animals that penetrate farthest into the marsh are among those that burrow in the mud.

Several kinds of polychaetes, relatives of clam worms, live in the mudbanks. They leave a glistening trail of mucus behind them as they burrow through the soft mud in search of food. One of these annelids resembles a small, dark red earthworm and can be found living in vertical burrows which open out in little mud cones built up above the marsh surface.

Mya, the soft-shell clam, and *Mercenaria,* the

quahog, as well as smaller species, dig into the soft muds and sands. Hermit crabs drag their borrowed shells about on the surface of the mud. Under the wandering crabs, snapping shrimp dig their way into the soft mud surface at low water. Occasionally, you can hear a loud pop when one of these small shrimp snaps his claw shut past the catch that holds it open.

Some of these animals, mostly water dwellers, can stand little air exposure. None can withstand the exposure to which they would be subject up in the marsh proper. Only in a marsh pool can they be found much above low tide level. To have the good life, they must choose a pool that is flooded by almost every high tide. The flooding prevents the salinity from being greatly diluted by rains, which might prove fatal, or being increased by evaporation, which might have the same disastrous effect.

These tide pools are the best places for the lazy observer to catch up on his small animal watching, since you can walk up to the edge of the pool at low tide when the ground is not wet and see through the quiet water surface. In a good pool you may see paired dark holes in the mud, which indicate that there is a clam below, his siphons open, circulating water through his shell-encased body. You might even be lucky enough to see a slight mound which forms the center of a set of thin, light-colored tentacles which resemble elastic threads. Bits of mud and sandy material move along the tentacles to the mouth at the center of a lovely red Amphitrite hiding in the mud.

Fish dart from one side to the other, making small disturbances in the pool. *Fundulus heteroclitus,* the mummichog, is common throughout the marshes from the Gulf of St. Lawrence to the Gulf of Mexico. *Fundulus majalis,* the banded killifish, is found from Cape Cod south, as is the sheepshead minnow, *Cyprinidon variegatus.* The males of this chubby little minnow assume bright colors during breeding season. *Gambusia affinis,* the top minnow, lives from New Jersey south.

*Salt marsh minnows: killifish; top minnow; sheepshead;
mummichog*

The top minnow is viviparous, that is, bears its young
alive. The female is two and a half inches long, not
large by minnow standards, and bears about twenty-five
young which are one third of an inch long. The males
rarely grow to as much as one inch in length, but the
species makes up in fecundity and pugnaciousness what
it lacks in size. One of the principal foods of this small
fish is mosquito larvae, so the pools in which these and
other less common marsh minnows live are nearly free
of mosquito larvae. The slow-moving, fully exposed larvae have little chance to avoid the agile fish. Mosquitoes are successful only in the very temporary pools
higher up toward land, which the fish cannot reach.

The tide pools are also inhabited by the ghostly
shrimp, *Crangon,* only about one inch long. It may be
found from Labrador to Florida. Other little shrimps in
the genus *Palaeomonetes,* which also has a number of
freshwater species, occur in the marsh pools from Massachusetts to Texas.

Moving up toward land, away from these animals
which must be underwater most or all of the time, is the
beginning of the marsh proper, the dwelling place of
animals that depend on *Spartina* for their existence.

In the tall grass that grows along the creeks on the
edges of the marsh occur a number of estuarine animals

that live at lower tidal levels but sometimes make their way a short distance up into the marsh proper. The mud snail, *Nassarius obsoletus,* crawls up to feed on diatoms growing on the mud surface where the grass is not so dense as to shade them out. Hordes of these little black snails, moving along at low tide, can change the color of the mud from golden-brown, diatom-caused hue to natural gray-brown in a few minutes.

Small blue crabs, *Callinectes sapidus,* can be found hiding in the mud at low tide, waiting for the water to rise so they can swim about again and search for food. Their close but nonswimming relative, the green crab *Carcinus maenas,* may live in large holes dug in soft areas. The bottoms of their burrows are usually wet even at low tide. They, too, come out at high water to eat whatever sort of animal food they can get their claws on.

Blue crab

Panopeus herbstii and *Eurypanopeus depressus,* two small mud crabs that are abundant low in the tidal zone, also move up into the edge of the marsh. They may make permanent burrows in which they hide at low tide.

A few typically estuarine animals penetrate even farther into the marsh. The clam worm, *Neanthes,* is found everywhere, burrowing through mud and muddy sand. In the southern marshes, a relative, *Laeonereis,* can be found even up on the salty sand flats which are flooded only at high tides. The lack of dense plant growth for cover makes *Laeonereis* easy prey for shorebirds and waders who probe the marsh for food. The little blood-red earthworm-like polychaete, *Capitella capitata,* is sometimes very abundant in the soft muds.

Amphipods are found at the base of *Spartina* stalks and under dead stalks. These laterally compressed crustacea, commonly called beach or sand hoppers, occur

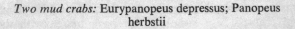

Two mud crabs: Eurypanopeus depressus; Panopeus herbstii

throughout the marsh. Although the species in the wet areas are different from those up near land, all these little gray-green hoppers look very much alike to the casual observer. They are an important item in the diet of the sharp-tailed sparrow.

The diamond-backed terrapin can also be fairly abundant in the southern and middle Atlantic marshes from which it was once taken in tremendous numbers for food. They were so abundant that there were restrictions as to the frequency with which they and another present-day delicacy, lobster, could be served to indentured servants. The servants objected to being served such common food more than a few times a week.

Diamond-backed terrapin

High tide brings swimming visitors from the sea to the marsh. Young game fish and tiny squid may move in to hunt between the grass stems. Bottlenose porpoises occasionally nose about in the soft mud for clams and crabs. These swimmers go back to sea with the

receding water. As they are not at all adapted for life
out of water, they die if caught too high in the marsh on
a falling tide.

The salt marsh is intertidal and becomes progressively higher in the tidal zone as it develops. The flats
might have been exposed to the air and sun for only
short periods at each tide. The marsh is exposed for
more than half of the time, since it lies almost entirely
above the midtide level. It is exposed to freshwater
dilution during rains. It is exposed to devastating drying
during days of low humidity. It is exposed to heat on
sunny days. It is more landlike than the nearby flats,
that are lower in the intertidal region, but it is not
entirely suitable for land animals adapted to exposure
to sun and air who are not used to having their habitat
inundated by salty water twice a day. Though the presence of tall plants growing up above the mud offers
advantages over the bare sand flats that precede the
marsh, the marsh is a more difficult place in which to
live.

Great changes in conditions occur in the salt marsh
and many organisms are not adapted to cope with such
changes. This is reflected in the fact that relatively few
species of animals live in the salt marsh, and even more
so in the distribution of those that do. Most of them
avoid the greatest changes by living either primarily on
the land and in the air, or under the water.

The first group is composed largely of insects and
spiders, along with some larger animals such as raccoons, swamp rabbits, mice, otters, and various birds,
which have invaded the marsh from the landward edge.
They are typically land dwellers, some of which go only
into the most landward parts of the marsh. Others go
all the way across the marsh to the edges of the tidal
creeks. Many of these leave the marsh or crawl up the
grass stems at each high tide and so manage to avoid
many of the problems associated with living in the sea.

The aquatic group, mollusks, worms, and crustaceans, lives near the low tide region of the marsh and

hides in the mud during the period when the tide is out. There are only a few animals that are abundant on the marsh itself and even fewer that manage to be active both in and out of water.

Most of the species of terrestrial invaders are insects: grasshoppers, which eat the *Spartina* in the southern marshes; crickets, which inhabit the more northern *S. patens* marshes; plant hoppers, which suck the sap from *Spartina* leaves and stalks; and flies with sponging mouthparts that feed on plant secretions and detritus, the decomposed bits of marsh plants lying about the surface soils.

Ants occur frequently, especially in the more landward parts on local high spots which are not often flooded. Beetles share the densely vegetated high areas with the crickets where the previous year's dead grass provides snug cover. Thousands of springtails are also bedded in this area and are the prey of a tiny, blind pseudoscorpion less than a quarter of an inch long.

Dragonflies, predatory flies, beetles, and bugs, along with numerous spiders, hunt the herbivorous insects. Larvae of flies live in the mud and in the stems of *Spartina*. Larvae of parasitic wasps live in the bodies of other insects. At least four hundred kinds of insects have been found living in salt marshes. Only a few of these are abundant and perhaps fifty are characteristic of the marshes, being found there in larger numbers than in any other habitat.

Among these are a few that have been studied in some detail and about which we will say more later. In this small group is *Orchelium fidicinium,* a grasshopper that lives on *Spartina alterniflora*. It is one of the few large insects found living in the salt marsh throughout its life cycle. Another is the plant hopper, *Prokelisia marginata,* which sucks the juices of the *Spartina* plants. It may be so abundant that it occasionally darkens the *Spartina* leaves along the creek banks.

The biting flies have attracted attention because of the nuisance they make of themselves. The tabanids, or greenheads, with their fierce blood-drawing bites, the smaller salt marsh mosquito, *Aedes sollicitans,* and the sand flies or biting midges, *Ceratopogonids,* substitute in numbers for what they lack in size. The less objectionable, man-avoiding insects have stirred up little trouble for themselves, but they fall victim to the changes men have visited upon the marshes in their efforts to do the biting flies to death.

The larvae of all these pesty insects are true marsh dwellers. Greenhead larvae live in the mud throughout the marsh. Mosquito larvae, the active wrigglers whose bodies can be so numerous that they give a black hue to water, live in isolated pools. Biting midge larvae live in the ground but prefer the sandier parts of the marsh near land.

Other flies are even more abundant than the ones whose habits bring them so unpleasantly to attention. The most common marsh flies belong to the family *Chloropidae,* named for the green eyes of many species. These are tiny flies only two or three millimeters long, usually black in color. They are so small that they escape attention except when they gather in swarms like wisps of smoke over the marsh. The larvae of most live in stems of grass and eat the grass tissue. One, called the frit fly, is among the most important pests of grain in Europe and many in the family infest cereal and pasture grasses. The frit fly larvae live as stem miners in barley in the fall and early spring, but the summer generation lives in the developing grain. The empty

Three mud flies: greenhead; biting midge; deerfly

kernels resulting from their attack are called "frits" in Sweden, hence, the name.

This species, *Oscinella frit,* isn't found in the marsh, but other members of the same genus are abundant. The marsh species probably attacks *Spartina.* We have seen empty kernels on the seed stalks.

Other members of this abundant family live as larvae in decaying vegetation rather than living stems. The genus *Hippelates* are called eye gnats for the habit of alighting on moist parts of the body surface, around the eyes, and on wounds. They can be a great nuisance and were among the first insects recognized as disease carriers.

Very little is known about the habits, life histories, or importance of these little flies to the marshes. In fact, very little is known about any of the marsh insects other than those that attack people or are very large and conspicuous. Anyone willing to make careful observations, to wait with patience for nature to perform, and to spend a little time reading the little that is already known, can make considerable contributions to science even though he has no scientific training himself. The animals are there to study. The way they fit into the marsh system is almost unknown. Some of them may be important. At least the more abundant ones must be significant in the marsh economy.

The members of the land and air group, spiders and insects, are arthropods or jointed-leg animals. The arthropods wear their skeletons outside their bodies as a protective covering; they are the most abundant multicellular animals on earth, the insects on land and the crustaceans in the water. It is not surprising that these should have been the creatures to invade the marsh from two sides, the land and water.

Because their skin is covered by their skeletons, arthropods can easily limit the extent to which their body fluids interact with the fluids around them. So, insects and spiders can avoid problems of water and salt bal-

Eye gnat

ance by shutting themselves off from the seawater which wets them on the marsh.

No animal can shut itself off entirely from its environment and continue to live. It must breathe, eat, and get rid of wastes. Living organisms can only take materials into their bodies and push waste products out through moist membranes.

We breathe through the moist membranes of our lungs, which are tucked inside our chest cavity. The lungs are kept safe and warm but, nevertheless, expose a vast area of moist membrane to air. We take our food in through a membrane which lines our digestive tract. The membrane is inside our body for protection and because it is much more convenient to carry our meal with us while we digest it rather than perform the whole operation outside the body. Yet the real limit of our body is the lining of the tract, and the content of our stomach is inside us only as much as the space in the hole of a doughnut is inside the doughnut. The space within the tube that forms our digestive tract and the doughnut's hole are topologically identical. The content of the tract contacts the cells and body fluids only through the wet membrane that lines the digestive tract.

All this is simply to say that to live, any animal's body cells must have intimate contact with the outside world. But the area of contact may be limited. Marine animals, other than vertebrates, have less need than others for a waterproof skin because they are in osmotic balance with seawater.

Land animals, on the other hand, run the constant risk of drying. A waterproof skin is a valuable asset and was one of the early steps taken in the evolution of land animals. Since they are not in contact with water most of the time, they get their salts from food and drink their water from freshwater supplies or get it from that which is produced within their bodies as a by-product of their metabolism. Insects and spiders develop their skeleton into a very nearly waterproof covering and occupy almost all land habitats. About the only change that was necessary for many of them to invade the marsh was to adapt their behavior to marsh conditions. They live in normal insect ways while the tide is out. When the tide rises, the more active fliers, such as some of the flies and beetles, simply fly to local high spots. Many of the other larger insects crawl up the grass stems and so can stay above all but the highest tides.

The smallest insects can rest on the surface film of the water and hop onto any solid grass they may come to as they ride along with the wind: Some are small enough to live within the hollow grass stems where air is always present.

Even large insects will not necessarily drown when covered by water for short periods. Their skin is waterproof, so water on their body covering does no harm. They breathe, as do spiders, through tiny tubes and passages that carry the air in to all parts of the body. Only the very tips of these air passages are not waterproofed and can pass air and water through their walls. But the openings to the tubes are both tiny and waterproofed, and sometimes have valves with which they can be closed. Even if the tubes are open, water cannot enter them as it cannot wet the walls. The breathing system doesn't get wet even though the insect is underwater. Insects can be very active creatures, but when necessary, they can sit quietly without using much oxygen. They survive the short period at high tide while waiting for air to find its way back to them.

Some of the insects are more closely associated with seawater in the marsh, especially as larvae. The maggot stages of the fierce-biting greenheads and of the biting midges live in the salty ground. They cannot escape the sea any more than can the mosquito larvae which live in the marsh pools. These insects must have solved the problem of controlling the salt concentrations of their body fluids before they successfully invaded the salt marsh. They use their impervious exoskeletons advantageously and restrict exchange to the areas of their gut and gills, if any.

The excess salts that do get into the body are excreted by their excretory glands, which have a greater capacity for salt secretion than do those of their freshwater relatives. It takes an effort to excrete these salts. Energy must always be used to push salts from the less to the more concentrated solution. This is the reason that freshwater made from seawater is expensive. The

Mosquito wriggler and greenhead maggot

restriction of the area through which the salts can enter the larvae's bodies enables the larvae to spend less energy on salt secretion and be more efficient in the use of food energy.

Moving from the small, hard-to-see animals to the large-scale beasts that are noticed and familiar, you can find birds characteristic of the marsh. Long-billed marsh wrens live along the creeks where the tall grass forms a forest for these diminutive birds. The lower *Spartina alterniflora,* in back of the creeks, is the chosen habitat of the seaside sparrow, while the secretive sharp-tailed sparrows live even farther up toward land and hide in *S. patens* meadows. Clapper rails choose areas of dense *S. alterniflora* where their thin-as-a-rail shape permits them to slip between the grass stems. Harriers or marsh hawks nest on local high spots and hawk up and down the flat ground looking for prey.

There are many other birds that can usually be found on the marsh but for whom the marsh is not their characteristic habitat. Black ducks and blue-winged teal nest on the salt marsh, especially where there are ponds. Short-eared owls are attracted by broad open spaces where they like to hunt. They may nest on a hummock or rock protruding from the marsh. American bitterns use the salt marshes but are more characteristically found in freshwater marshes. Redwings, boat-tailed and common grackles may nest in the taller grasses but they are not as successful there as they are in freshwater marshes where the water level does not rise and fall with the tides. Birds usually found on upland meadows, such as Savannah sparrows and meadowlarks, take advantage of the *S. patens* resemblance to their upland habitat. Song sparrows, catbirds, and yellowthroats occur in shrubby borders of the marsh and on the tidal area where there is a thick growth of marsh elder.

Large numbers of birds rest and feed on the marshes in the winter. Virginia rails, herons, curlews, sandpipers, plovers, ducks, and geese make use of the marsh

Long-billed marsh wren at nest

while they are migrating. Some individuals may remain all winter.

Raccoons commonly come into the marsh to dig for clams and crabs and may stay for days on end, especially in summer. Rice rats live in marshlands in the south; white-footed mice in the north. Otters are seen swimming in the creeks and loping across the grass as they move from one creek to another. They are delightful show-offs and will put on an hour-long exhibition of gay frolic if their audience is quiet enough. Mink regularly visit the marsh to feed. If they can find a suitable high spot or hollow log washed up on the marsh, they may build a nest of *Spartina* where they bear and rear their young. This requires a stay of about two months, which makes the mink an important predator to any area that has a family in residence.

Birds and mammals, which are essentially terrestrial groups, solve the salt problem in a manner similar to that used by insects. Their skin is relatively, though not completely, waterproof. They have developed the ability to excrete salts from a less to a more concentrated solution. Neither group excretes salts directly into the sea, however, The excess salts which they get in food and from seawater swallowed with food are excreted into a cavity within the body and pushed outside from there.

Mammals excrete into their urine as it is being formed in the kidneys. Humans cannot make urine with more salts in it than are in the blood and we cannot drink seawater without either drinking even more freshwater to wash the salts out again, or dying. A number of small mammals, including salt marsh mice, can make concentrated urines so they survive on the marsh without having to leave in search of freshwater.

Birds excrete excess salt by means of special glands associated with their noses, called nasal glands or salt glands. Brine is blown out with expired air or drips from the end of the beak. The characteristic headshake of the gull is used to get rid of briny droplets.

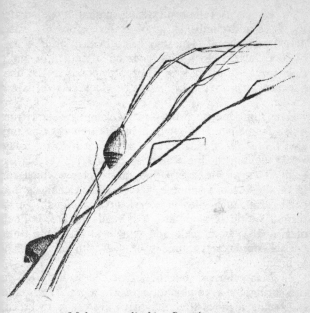

Melampus *climbing* Spartina *stem*

Turtles, which are also found in the salt marsh, have salt glands which excrete excess salt into the eyes. The "tears," which marine turtles shed when coming ashore to lay their eggs, are the work of these glands. They also "weep" while in seawater, but the droplets are never seen because they are immediately washed away.

Snails thrive in the upper parts of the marsh. *Melampus* tends to stay in damp areas, under the grass at low tide when there is a hot sun, as it has no operculum, a horny dish with which it can close its shell. As the tide rises, *Melampus* climbs grass stalks. Since it is a pulmonate snail, that is, has a lung, it can take a breath of air if the tide rises high enough to submerge it. With this last breath, it can last for an hour or so, until the tide drops.

Melampus is rather surprising in that it anticipates the tides and climbs the grass stalks before the water actually reaches it. The snail has a built-in cycle, a sort of inner alarm clock, that goes off after a little more than twelve hours passes. This corresponds to the time between successive tides. How the clock gets set is not known.

The reproductive process of *Melampus* differs from other pulmonate snails which hatch from eggs as tiny snails. *Melampus* hatches as a larva that lives for a few weeks floating in the water, as does a typical marine snail. This provides a period of travel by which the larva can reach a suitable marsh. It then changes into snail form and settles in a high area of marsh. In its second spring of snail life, it is ready to breed. Each individual is both male and female at the same time, but self-sterile, and so must still meet with another snail to breed.

In Massachusetts marshes, breeding is triggered in the spring by a combination of warming waters and shortening nights. After the snails are ready to breed, they wait until a day or so after the biweekly highest or spring tides to congregate in masses on the stems of *Spartina*. They breed, lay their eggs and disperse, all within a few days. The eggs are deposited in a gelatinous mass without much protection against drying except that which is provided by the grass and the detritus deposited on the eggs by the spring tides. Two weeks later, at the next spring tide, the snails congregate and breed again.

Even if taken into the laboratory they will congregate at the proper time in relation to the tides on their particular marsh. They will do this even in the middle of winter and without any external clue as to state of tide, as long as the temperature and night length are suitable.

We are not certain how they know that the proper time has arrived, but there is an indication that they have a second internal clock that runs on a twenty-

Marsh periwinkle on Spartina *stem*

four-hour schedule. Every time their daily clock is in phase with their tidal clock, another two weeks has passed and another spring tide has arrived.

Another snail, *Littorina irrorata,* is fairly common as far north as Massachusetts, but is more abundant in southern marshes. Its rocky shore relative, *L. littorea,* the common periwinkle, replaces it on the marshes of New England and the Canadian Maritimes. These snails are basically marine and have made few special adaptations to marsh living, although they have invaded the marsh extensively. Unlike *Melampus,* they do have a horny operculum which they can draw into the opening of their shells to seal themselves against drying during low tide periods.

The ribbed mussel, *Modiolus demissus,* which resembles in outline the common mussel found on rocky coasts, lives buried up to its middle in marsh mud. It is quite common along the creek levees and in other areas where the tide floods the marsh regularly. The ribbed mussel is a filter feeder, straining all manner of particles out of the water, swallowing the edibles and rejecting the inedibles, bound together in a ribbon of mucus and mud, called pseudofeces. These pseudofeces accumulate in large amounts where the currents are too weak to wash them away from the clumps of mussels. The mussels literally bury themselves in this by-product of their feeding activities and have to keep moving upward to stay alive. A marsh acquires a hummocky appearance, with the height of the hummocks limited to the level at which the mussels can extract enough food from the tides to stay alive.

All of these mollusks can stand long periods with reduced oxygen and are not in danger from the buildup of metabolic acids as they have a large supply of limy shell with which they can neutralize them. They can also expose themselves by opening slightly to obtain oxygen from the air if they do not expose themselves to much drying in doing so. This ability to close also protects them from osmotic damage by freshwater. Marine mollusks probably have little ability to adjust to osmotic changes in their environment. When the environment is unsuitable, they close it out. They can keep it out for remarkably long periods and still survive. We have kept *Littorina* dry, in a bottle on a shelf, for several months. They all emerged in good condition when put back into the water.

From Virginia south to the mangroves lives a clam, *Polymesoda caroliniana,* inhabiting an oval shell from one to two inches in diameter, covered by a greenish, shining outer layer. This little clam is typical of brackish water at the mouths of rivers and may be abundant in the salt marshes of such regions, even in places which are not flooded for days at a time.

At least one filter-feeding polychaete worm lives in the marsh muds, a tiny animal only a tenth of an inch long. Very little water is needed to provide it with its own small tidepool for private feeding.

All of these animals pass their larval stage in the sea, but there are a few others which spend their entire life within the marsh. At least two genuine earthworms have invaded the marsh. They are pink-white creatures nearer the size of a pencil lead than the pencil-sized night crawlers you can see taking the air on top of the soil after a summer rain.

The number of earthworm species is uncertain as they are extremely difficult to identify. The worms have no difficulty among themselves, but they undoubtedly rely on a chemical sense in sorting each other out, rather than on sight as we do.

There are a few amphipods which live and raise their young in the marsh. Some insects live as larvae in the marsh, but the adults are essentially land creatures that avoid the water as much as possible.

Of all the grassy marsh animals mentioned, and the hundreds not mentioned, there are only a half dozen or so who spend their entire lives there. There are a dozen or so more who live their adult lives completely integrated into this half-wet, half-dry, changeable environment.

Among these, the best adapted are the fiddler crabs, *Uca pugilator* and *Uca pugnax,* and the related square backed crabs, *Sesarma cinereum* and *Sesarma reticulatum.* These crabs are derived from marine ancestors and are still tied to the sea in their larval stages. When the eggs carried by the female are ready to hatch, she makes her way to the water's edge into which the young float, carried by tidal currents, until they are ready to settle down as tiny crabs on some suitable marsh.

The drifting larvae often fail to reach a suitable place and perish, as do many more that are eaten, before they have a chance to change into adult form. The drifting stage is a benefit as well as a disadvantage. Most of the larvae die before they can find a marsh on which to settle. But their drifting existence disperses them so widely along the shores that virtually no suitable marsh will fail to be discovered and colonized.

Of the square-backed crabs, *Sesarma cinereum* lives in the landward and higher portions of the marsh. It seems to be a considerable way toward becoming a land animal. *Sesarma reticulatum*, a heavy-bodied crab, lives in large burrows in the muddy parts of the marsh.

Both specific names of the abundant fiddler crabs, *Uca pugilator* and *Uca pugnax*, refer to the fighting nature of the males, whose single large claw and territorial behavior during the breeding season attract a great deal of attention. They move their bodies and wave their big claws with a definite rhythm. If a lady crab is enticed by the display, the two crabs retire into the male's burrow. Later, the female lays her eggs and carries them on her abdomen until they are ready to hatch.

The fiddler crabs have evolved several structures or mechanisms which fit them for marsh life. Under the edges of their shells, just above the legs, where other crabs carry only gills, the fiddlers have developed a primitive lung. As long as the crabs keep the cavity moist, this lung can serve for breathing in air. Since the fiddlers retire into burrows to wait out difficult periods of high tides and cold seasons, they have also developed the ability to withstand extended periods without oxygen. They store up the mildly poisonous lactic acid that is produced during life processes without oxygen and

Fiddler crabs

rebuild a portion of it back into useful energy stores as glycogen or animal starch upon their return to air.

They have a highly developed water and salt control system so that they not only can live in diluted seawater and still maintain their internal environment constant, as can most estuarine animals, but they can also regulate their body fluids when in contact with concentrated seawater, a rarer accomplishment. This permits them to hunt for food in the briny pools concentrated by the summer sun on high areas of marsh at periods of lower high tides.

The fiddlers feed on large pieces of animals which may come their way or on the tiny plants, animals, and plant remains that litter the surface mud. Here the species differ slightly. *Uca pugilator,* which lives on sand, has special spoon-shaped hairs which enable it to sort food from sand, while its relative, *Uca pugnax,* living in the muddier parts, has feather-like hairs to handle the mud more efficiently.

To a certain extent, the *Uca* can compensate for changes in temperature. They can keep about the same level of activity from 58° to 80° F. Above 80°, their metabolism speeds up rapidly. At slightly higher temperatures, they die. Below 58° they slow down very rapidly and quickly go into a torpor. When temperatures fall to these low limits, they retire into their burrows where they are safe from predators while they are in a slow-moving condition.

They act somewhat like small mammals that go into hibernation at low temperatures. The crabs maintain a constant level of activity at high temperatures except that they control their metabolism, keeping it constant in spite of changing temperature, rather than controlling their internal temperature, which in turn results in a constant metabolism.

The earthworms mentioned before are rarities in the marsh in that they evolved from freshwater ancestors. All animals have internal fluids that are saltier than freshwater. So freshwater animals evolved mechanisms to collect salts from the very dilute solution in which they live and keep them inside once they have collected them. Animals living in freshwater do not need waterproof skins since water will move into their bodies and they use what they need and excrete the extra in their urine. Since their skin is not waterproof, gases will also pass through it. They can breathe through their skin as do frogs and toads.

Because of these provisions for water and salt balance, a freshwater animal is the least suited to invade a salt marsh. Its surface will allow its body fluids to lose water to the more concentrated sea, the sea salts will leak in, and the net result will be a fatal increase of salts within the body. Though the earthworms have made the adjustment, they would seem to have started with the odds against them.

Fish have also entered the sea from freshwater where they evolved. Fish do not have a permeable skin and would seem better able to make the transition than would earthworms or freshwater snails. But fish must breathe and eat and so are not completely isolated, osmotically, from the water in which they swim.

The blood of fish and of the rest of the vertebrates which evolved from them is about one third as concentrated as seawater. Fish gain water and lose salts in freshwater; lose water and gain salts in the sea. In freshwater they secrete large quantities of urine to rid themselves of extra water. Salts lost with the water are replaced from food and by special salt-absorbing cells on their gills. When they entered the sea, bony fish reduced their kidneys to lessen urine production. Necessary water is obtained from drinking seawater. The seawater is absorbed in the intestine and the salts are then secreted through the gills. Many of the marsh-dwelling fish, the mummichog for example, retain the ability to regulate their osmotic concentration throughout the range from freshwater to full seawater.

To the south, there is an entirely new group of animals that appear in the mud-water-tree mixture of the mangrove swamps. The swamps offer living spaces for a very intimate mixture of animal types typical of mud flats, rock shores, shallow seas, and tropical forests. The water animals come and go with the tides or remain in the pools that are trapped at low tide.

The mud flat animals have a nearly ideal spot for existence. It is soft, for there is no mat of fine roots to bind it, as in the grassy marshes. The mud is easily penetrated by the soft-bodied creatures that rely on it for protection and as a dwelling place. The evergreen forest above protects the area from the intense tropical sun. Problems of high temperature and low humidity are minimized.

The soft mud provides little support for an attached animal, but just above its surface is a tangle of roots, prop roots, and breathing roots which are solid and fixed. These offer ideal support for fixed animals. Here is a damp, shaded, solid, intertidal habitat that extends for miles, the counterpart of the little rock crevices that

*Mangrove swamp inhabitants: coon oysters; periwinkles;
clapper rail; little blue heron; egret; spoonbills*

shelter intertidal animals along rocky coasts. Finally,
there are the stems and crowns of the trees, a habitat
more terrestrial than marine. During tropical storms,
the tree habitat becomes a mixture of finely divided
wind and seawater that immerses everything.

Each part of the mangrove swamp supports its own

type of creature. Clusters of mangrove or coon oysters, *Ostrea frons,* cling to the prop roots; the heavy ridges of the shells extend around and clasp their supports. Small crabs and several varieties of worms creep in the crevices between the oysters. Barnacles and mussels compete for space on the roots. Mangroves have their representative of the tough, periwinkle tribe. *Littorina angulifera* crawls on the stems and roots above the oysters. A number of hydroids, tunicates, and sponges live below, next to the damp mud. Amphipods occur everywhere. Fiddler and mud crabs, snapping shrimp, and worms burrow in the soft mud.

Clapper rails and the ubiquitous raccoon crawl over the roots, or swim between them, along with diamond-backed terrapin, water moccasins, and in the southern-most part, an occasional American crocodile.

The red mangrove water snake crawls about in the branches and prop roots, along with a less conspicuous, black variant. Both drape themselves over branches along the creeks to take the sun and surprise visitors who fail to notice them until, disturbed, they drop into the water and swim away. These nonpoisonous snakes are close relatives of and grade into the salt marsh snakes, two subspecies which occur in *Spartina* marshes along the Gulf Coast and the north coast of Florida. All water snakes have bad reputations from their spirited self-defense, for they strike and bite fiercely when cornered. They are excellent swimmers and feed on small fish and crabs.

In shallow pools, between clusters of black mangroves, live the killifish, including the viviparous sail-finned killifish, *Mollineisia lattipinna;* the brilliant display colors of the male rival or surpass those of the sheepshead minnow, another resident. Water boatmen, back swimmers, beetles and midge larvae abound, as do small shrimp. All of these small animals furnish food for the large colonies of wading birds that nest in the tops of the mangroves.

Up in the treetop habitat, more terrestrial than marine, an incredible congregation of water birds nest: little blue herons, Louisiana herons, snowy and common egrets, and white ibis. The mangrove beneath the nesting birds is covered with the white snow of their droppings. In a few places, there may even be a few of the beautiful and shy birds, the roseate spoonbills.

Life in the tropics is abundant, for conditions are favorable and relatively uniform. Organisms are not put to the test as often as they are where variations are greater or more frequent. Tropical animals' difficulties are more likely to be with their neighbors than with the climate in which they live.

10. The Seasons of the Marsh

THE SEA RISES INTO THE TIDAL CREEKS AND FLOODS over the marsh at dawn, at midday, at dusk, by moonlight, as the revolving of the moon and the revolving of the earth change step.

During the cold months of the year, the tide may rise with ice on its surface but still be warmer than the mud. In midsummer it may be warm, but still cooler than the mud surface which has been heated by the sun. The moderation of climate produced by the sea results from this slowness of the water temperature to change with the seasons. The moderation of the water temperature makes abrupt changes in marsh temperatures when the tide rises and falls. All animal life in the marsh must adjust to these changes.

It adjusts by physiological, chemical, and structural adaptations, as well as behavioral adaptations made to cope with the seasonal changes. The more northern the marsh, the less difference the tide makes to animals in the winter. They are all resting, made torpid by the cold, or have departed to take refuge in warmer places. Crabs have retreated down into the mud, too cold to respond to any stimuli. Insects rest as eggs or larvae in the mud, or are burrowed in the ground above the high tide mark as adults. The birds have gone south. Mummichogs have buried themselves in the mud, in the pools and creeks that do not dry up, and so avoid exposure to ice. Raccoons may still come out occasionally to fish,

hoping to find a clam, or a crab too cold to protest a
being eaten.

At high tide, a few hardy fish may come in to the
edges of the marsh to feed. Their catch is meager. The
autumn activity has slowed down dramatically. Winter
is the time of leanness. The waters of the estuaries tend
to be at their clearest. Sunlight comes farther into the
water than it did in summer and the water is full of
nutrients from the decay of the summer's produce. Phytoplankton blooms. The animal plankton feeds on the
phytoplankton and grows abundant. Any fish still trying
to feed from the marsh abandon the effort and turn
their attention to the water.

Not only the animals, but the plants are affected by
the cold. If the winter is severe enough to freeze the
seawater and there are storms to push cakes of ice up
onto the frozen mud, anything protruding above the
surface will be ground to bits or sheared off and carried
out to decay in the sea. Even if there is no ice damage,
the stems and blades of the grasses are killed. Only the
underground parts can resist freezing. They remain protected in a blanket of wet or frozen mud, until the
spring sun warms the marsh.

Farther south, the winter is less important. The grass
may remain alive throughout the winter season, as it
does at the southern limits of the grassy marshes. Plant
hoppers dining on juices they tap from *Spartina* may be
abundant enough even in winter to darken the tips of
the grass blades they climb to escape high tide. In the
semitropical mangroves, the winter is much like the
summer, only a little less warm with less animal activity. But, even as far south as Georgia, the crabs go to
sleep for the winter.

The marsh in winter is a desolate sea of brown dead
grass or of mud with a short stubble. In Georgia, the
tall grass of last year hides the new green growth underneath, which begins in winter. Animal activity is restricted to the seawater where it is still comparatively
warm. Birds that have come south from much colder

climates rest in the warmth of the southern winter a short distance out to sea or on the outer shores.

Birds must have a continuous supply of food to keep their bodies warm. In the northern winter they cannot eat from the marsh except in the creeks. The northern bird population is restricted to ducks that feed in the water. They chase the fish slowed by cold and they poke and dab in the mud, sifting out the little worms and clams hiding there. Hunting up in the marsh is very poor for the ducks. The worms have gone deep in the mud, or the mud is frozen. Even if the mud is not frozen, dabbling is difficult, due to the root mat under the soil surface. Brant rest on the water and feed on eelgrass that grows below low tide level, around the edges of the marsh.

Animal life in the winter eases itself out of the marsh. Some inhabitants move away. Some burrow down deep. Some, that cannot move, stay as quiet as possible and survive until spring. A quietness settles everywhere. Snapping shrimp are silent. There are no loud territorial disputes between birds. Solitary herons fish the creeks. The fiddler crabs do not rustle through the plant stems.

As the season changes, spring seems to come while the tide is out and winter to creep back with the cold water of high tide. The flats and the marsh muds are warmed at low tide, for there is no tall grass to shade the surface. When the tide turns, the heat stored in the thin warmed layer of mud passes into the cold water that creeps up. The water is slightly warmed but then goes back and mixes with the great reservoir of cold water at the edge of the sea. Many sunny days must pass before the heat penetrates very far into the water. Maritime climates reflect this slow heating of the sea and explain why the forsythia blooms ten days later on Cape Cod than it does in Boston, sixty miles to the north.

Marsh animals may have a delayed spring or a spring that alternates with the tides. Low water at noon in

Ducks dabbling

March or April on a sunny, warming day may mean that the mud at the surface reaches temperatures of around 80° F. As the evening high tide covers the mud, the temperature abruptly falls to that of the water, somewhere below 40° F. At night, the cooled wet mud, cooled further by evaporation when the tide again recedes, may well go below freezing.

Most intermediate-sized animals are not aware of these violent temperature changes. They are safely buried some inches under the mud or the water and will not come out into the world until the warmth of spring, penetrating slowly deeper and deeper into the ground, finally arouses them to the surface.

But most of the activity of the marsh takes place at

the surface of the mud. The organisms involved in this activity are so small that we rarely think of them. These are animals, plants, and bacteria which account numerically for most of the marsh's organisms. They are concentrated at the mud surface and are subject to the full force of the difficulties that the marsh makes for its inhabitants. They are also the first recipients of its benefits.

The plants, one-celled diatoms and flagellates, grow in full sunlight on a solid surface where fertilizing nutrients are concentrated. Animals live at the surface where the plants grow and where any food settling from the water must come to rest. It is the ideal spot to find food, light, and the necessary elements for plant growth. But it is also the place most subject to changes in temperature as the sunlight comes and goes and the tides ebb and flow. It is subject to the full force of the cold spring rains which rinse away the salt and the full effect of the seawater which brings the salt back again.

Many of these minute plants and animals can move from an inch to a foot per hour. This is about as fast in relation to their body size as we walk in relation to ours. With even this slow rate of movement, they can retire into the mud and escape some of the harshest effects of the spring weather.

Bacteria cannot do much in the way of moving about. Many cannot move at all and others, which do move, progress very little in their lifetime—the time between the separation of the two halves of a dividing cell and the subsequent division of those resulting cells. A bacterium does not necessarily ever die but endlessly multiplies by dividing into two bacteria as long as growth is possible, unless destroyed by some force external to itself. Bacteria have been found in salt marsh muds with a lifetime so short that changes in their environment are practically nonexistent. The shortest known life cycle for any bacterium exists in *Pseudomonas natriegens*, which at 98° F. lives in the salt marsh muds less than ten minutes between divisions. Even the great changes in the spring temperatures would be slow in terms of such division rates.

In spite of setbacks, cold nights, gray, cold and rainy days, the mud does thaw and gradually warms up. With it the shallow parts of the sea, warmed to a significant extent by flowing up over mud and sand, also warm. Even the remnant icebergs that occasionally are grounded next to the most northern *Spartina* marshes eventually melt completely.

Plants begin to grow again. The mud on the creek banks turns a rich brown in the morning sun as the diatoms and dinoflagellates become abundant on the warmed mud. *Spartina* seeds, that escaped the birds and insects and fell into the mud the preceding fall, sprout. After a spring rain, they emerge to seek the sun. Some, not shaded by established plants, survive. *Salicornia* seeds sprout, even on salt areas, and begin to cover the bare spots on the marsh. Paths which summer fishermen trampled, killing the grasses, begin to turn green again as new shoots protrude from the rhizomes underground. Later, the shoots in the high marsh manage to push their way through the cover of last year's grass. The marsh begins to green up. The Fundy marshes turn from the red-brown of mud to green. New England high marshes change from gray to green, and southern marshes from brown grass and brown mud to light, fresh green.

The animals are also warmed and begin to be active again. Their food needs increase. The fiddler crabs suddenly appear aboveground when the temperature reaches about 60° F. in their holes. A larger relative of *Uca pugnax* and *U. pugilator, Uca minax,* doesn't come out of his hole in the river banks and fresher parts of the marsh until the temperature reaches 68° F.

The rising spring tides can be a critical time for some of the marsh inhabitants. They may be a bit less active than usual and fail to get into their burrows quickly enough when the cold water spills over them. Abruptly their movement is slowed. Gone is the advantage of having been warmed by the sun on a fine spring day.

The change in the marsh world, from air to water, is accentuated by the difference in temperature. Winter comes back abruptly. One moment a crab is moving about above the warm mud, his body warmed by sunlight and the mud. He moves easily through air which offers no resistance, breathing the abundant oxygen the air contains. He can see as well as stalked eyes can see, noticing any sudden movement within several feet of himself. Suddenly, or almost suddenly, this world changes. The crab is surrounded by water, perhaps twenty degrees colder than the air. Movement through the water is difficult even though it is at a crab's pace and is made harder still by the numbing effects of the cold surrounding the tiny limbs. Breathing becomes difficult. The water is probably full of oxygen, but water saturated with oxygen contains only one twentieth as much oxygen as does air. More work is necessary just to move enough water past the gills to extract necessary oxygen, although the cold which reduces the need for oxygen alleviates the problem somewhat. The water is harder to see through and provides cover and support for predators that swim in with the tide. So the crab is cautious and is seldom caught out when he cannot get back underground before getting inundated.

The sun continues to warm the edge of the land and the ribbon of green marshes is again seen along the coast. Male marsh wrens move in to the fast growing *Spartina* along the creek banks and begin staking out their territorial claims.

The male builds a nest and then another and another, weaving the leaves of *Spartina* into a hollow ball with an entrance at one side. One male may be content with three nests while his more energetic neighbor may build thirty. The earliest nests are made of dead, as well as fresh, leaves and are often pulled apart as the old leaves rot and the new continue to grow. It takes the male bird about ten hours of labor spread over several days to finish his nests. All this time, the grass is still growing. All of the later nests are framed with fresh, strong leaves. The last nests built survive for some time.

In spite of all this activity, the results are nothing to be proud of unless you take into consideration quantity. At best, the males' nests are incomplete and at worst only ridiculous parodies. Why the nests are built at all is a mystery. Perhaps it is simply a product of restless energy, or more likely, the multiple nests serve some courting function. Perhaps seeing the males' nests stimulates the female wren to exercise her nest-building instinct.

When the female is finally enticed by the singing of the male and his abilities at nest construction, she usually spurns his efforts to supply housing. She begins yet another nest but the male does most of the heavy construction as a dutiful husband should. When the female is satisfied with the nest shell, she lines it with shreds of grass, fallen feathers, and hairs shed by the marsh rats and raccoons. She also adds a sort of entrance tunnel which forms a sill to prevent the eggs or young from falling out of the nest. Finally, when she has begun to lay eggs, she plugs the entrance with a door of shredded leaves. This fine nest takes five to six days to complete.

The male nests are used no further, except, perhaps, as shelter for the night. Other animals may make use of them occasionally, also. *Sesarma cinereum*, the square-backed crab, hides in the old damp nests during the heat of the day. Paper wasps may use them as suitable places in which to build their own nests of paper. Rice rats find the nests just the right height and size to serve as a hide-a-way during the daylight sleeping hours. Occasionally, they may even bear their young in the old nests.

The marsh rails begin their nests hidden among the *Spartina*, but the nests are too heavy to be supported by the grass and rest on the ground although made of grass blades.

Sharp-tailed sparrows nest in small groups on even higher marsh areas. They often build right down in the weak grasses. Their nests are on the ground but must be above the level of the summer high tides or the young would drown. The nests are harder to find than one might think. Not only are they well hidden, but sharp-tailed sparrows are usually secretive. If the watcher remains quiet, the birds may move about readily and normally. If there is a disturbance, they hide themselves in the grass and disappear from view. Even when forced to fly, they go only a few feet before dropping back into the grass to conceal themselves again. When behaving normally, sharp-tails are more like mice in their movements than birds. They run through the grass with heads held low in front of them. Occasionally, they stretch up to look around and then go back to their running. More than one novice bird watcher has listed this bird as a mammal.

Sharp-tailed sparrow

An even more retiring marsh bird that begins nesting in the spring is the black rail. So secretive is this smallest of the rails that few bird watchers have even seen one. Their habits are only poorly known. It is generally believed that they are fairly widely distributed and perhaps even common, but since they are so elusive, this is only supposition. Cases are on record of nests being discovered by accident, carefully watched and approached with great caution in order to surprise the female on the nest. Each time the observer got to the nest, the female had already disappeared. The eggs were still warm, indicating that she had just left and was probably close by. The black rail is seen occasionally running mouselike through the *Spartina patens* marshes or flying heavily as if it were all he could do to stay a few feet above the grass.

These birds collect their food and that for their nestlings on the marsh. Insects from the *Spartina* and snails and crustaceans from the mud are taken. Seaside sparrows are said to be partial to small crabs while sharptails eat amphipods. Herbert Kale, who made an intensive study of the wrens in a Georgia marsh, pointed up the difference between the feeding habits of the sparrows and wrens by noting that he had never collected a wren with muddy feet nor a marsh sparrow with clean feet. The tiny snails that the wrens use as grit for grinding their food are apparently all taken from *Spartina* stems.

About the time the young birds hatch, insects become plentiful on the marsh. Plants seem to bloom with crops of sucking insects. Flies are everywhere on the mud between the growing plants at low tide. Grasshoppers hatch and begin to eat the tips of the leaves. Parasitic wasps look for hosts in which to lay their eggs. Mosquito larvae hatch and wriggle in the marsh pools looking for food and serving as food for various minnows and ducklings.

The tempo of life speeds up in the spring in the

marsh as it does on land, except that it is complicated by the tides, by the slowness with which water warms up in comparison with air, and by the changes in temperature and salinity as a result of the spring rains. It warms, nevertheless, and as summer advances, the activity of the marsh reaches its maximum. Growth and decay proceed at their greatest rates.

A dying grass blade in the lush growth along the creeks does not remain identifiable long. It is quickly decomposed by the bacteria when the temperature of the mud and water are at their summer height. The resulting detritus is eaten by a multitude of animals.

Summer is the season when the large biting greenhead flies abound in such numbers that they can be heard buzzing and bumping through the grass long before they are visible. But, if the flies are hunting for a blood meal, their approach can be so silent that the first warning of their presence is the sharp pain as they tear through skin to draw blood. A visit to the marsh in a bathing suit as the tide is turning and the wind dies can be maddeningly painful.

Closely related species of animals that live in the same area usually have readily apparent differences in habits. Ecologists argue as to whether they must have different habits to reduce competition if they are to continue living together, or whether it is simply a tendency by which the two species make fuller use of their environment. There are four common species of greenheads on the marshes. They show some differences in habits that are of importance. *Tabanus nigrovittatus* is the commonest. It doesn't venture far from the marshes, stays in the open, and is particularly unwilling to venture into woods. *T. lineola* leaves the marsh more readily and can be found in larger numbers close to bordering woods. The latter species prefers horses to people as a source of blood although it will stoop to attacking humans. The remaining two species are members of the genus *Chrysops*, usually called deerflies. These are quite ready to fly away from the marsh and pursue their victims into the woods. Although they are called deer-flies, they are not particular as to their prey.

As with the mosquitoes, it is only the female flies who bite to get the protein-rich blood meal needed to develop eggs. The males lack mandibles and feed on plant secretions. The males are retiring as well and fly only during the morning over open water or mud. The ladies are active all day. The males hover in groups, to which the females are attracted for mating. When one approaches, a male will fly at her with such violence that the thud of their contact is quite audible. Often, however, a male will miss the female entirely and return to his hovering position to await another chance. The adults live for several weeks and have plenty of time to mate successfully.

When her eggs are ready to be laid, the female places them on *Spartina* stalks or leaves, depending on the species. *Tabanus nigrovittatus* lays on the stems of *S. alterniflora*, about a foot above the mud. The larvae that hatch spend one or two years squeezing their leath-ery, telescoping bodies through the mud in a constant search for prey. They breathe air but can survive for several hours underwater and so survive the hundreds of high tides they encounter in a lifetime.

Summer is the spawning time for the salt marsh min-nows, the common and striped killifish, *Fundulus heter-oclitus* and *F. majalis*, the sheepshead minnow, *Cyprin-odon variegatus*, and the sticklebacks, of which the four-spined stickleback, *Apeltes quandracus*, is the most abundant. The first three species belong to the same family with similar breeding behavior.

As the sexual season approaches, the males begin to change color. The common killifish or mummichog is ordinarily a muddy green color without markings. The more streamlined striped killifish is the same color but has vertical black stripes on the male and horizontal stripes on the female. The very deep-bodied sheepshead is also dressed in olive drab most of the year.

The hints of color that can be imagined under the working uniform begin to intensify in the males. The killifish get darker, almost black on their backs, and their bellies become yellow. The mummichog looks steel blue along its sides. The fins of his cousin, the striped killifish, turn bright yellow. The little sheepshead does the best job in color transformation. His back becomes steel blue, his belly and fins yellow to orange edged with black.

All of these bright colors are for the benefit of the females, of course, and the males become quite cantankerous as they establish display areas in which to show off and attract the females. The colors can abruptly disappear when the fish is startled by the approach of a large animal or when a small male is attacked by a large one. The loss of the distinctive color changes the uniform of the smaller fish from "competing male—to be attacked" to "immature male or unready female—to be ignored." Presumably, the brightest and fiercest appearing at any moment gets the girl; clasps her with his fins while they shed eggs and milt simultaneously into shallow water. The spawning fish sweep the water with their tails, driving the sticky eggs toward the pebbles and *Spartina* stalks at the water's edge. There the eggs rest while they develop, to hatch during the high tide about two weeks later.

The sticklebacks don't leave their breeding so nearly to chance. The males build a nest of plant fragments stuck together with mucus secretions. They then display their breeding colors, consisting of reddish bellies and ventral fins, to the females and entice them into spawning in or near the nest. The male picks up the eggs, puts them into the nest, and guards them for a week or so, during which time they develop and hatch. The male even guards the fry until they can shift for themselves.

Summer is the breeding season for the crabs, too. You can watch the dance of the fiddlers for hours. The cumbersome large fiddle sported by the males, which is useless for eating and awkard for locomotion, suddenly becomes useful. With it the male attracts the female and defends his territory. Occasionally, one of the larger *Uca minax* kills one of his smaller relatives with his large claw. Whether he kills for food, or kills in defending his territory and then eats the fallen crab because it is there, is anyone's guess. Clearly, the large claw functions mostly in the summer during the mating season.

The three species of fiddlers have different patterns of motions that are recognized by the females seeking mates and by other males of the species. *Uca minax*, the largest crab, stands on his back legs and holds his fiddle halfway in the air, then suddenly waves it up as far as possible and jerks it back down in several stages. *Uca pugnax* holds his fiddle in front of his mouth, raises himself up off the ground slightly and moves the fiddle diagonally upward, then returns it with several jerks. When females are present, he also curtseys to them, moving his body up and down. *Uca pugilator* starts his display with his elbow up and the tip of the fiddle near the ground. Then he moves it up and out while standing on tiptoe and returns smoothly to his original position. When excited he will also pound his fist on the ground, so to speak, doing it with enough force so that it can be heard.

The division between a sandy and a muddy area in summer, where all three species are present, is quite a bobbing and waving place. Hundreds of males stand by their burrows and wave, their eyes raised high on their stalks, looking for a passing female or a trespassing male. The bowing and leading of possible brides into the burrow alternates with rushing at nearby males and fighting battles with the large claw. The battles are push and grab affairs without much serious damage to either individual, usually. A sudden movement by an observer, or a passing animal, sends the crabs into the openings of the burrows, soon to return to their dance once their extended eyes can see no further danger.

The mating dance is interrupted by the rising tide. For the *Uca pugilator,* which selects sandy creek banks

Uca pugnax *male*

as his home, the rising tide is an important signal of impending danger. When the tide is out and the bank exposed, the crabs are feeding or courting. The holes are visible, scattered over the bank surface. If it is not the mating season, *Uca pugnax* will be feeding with the *U. pugilator*. *U. pugnax* simply goes home to his grassy neighborhood where he continues to feed underwater. *U. pugilator* is in a more serious predicament. His hole, dug in sand, will not hold together when the water rises as does that of his relative who has dug in firmer mud. The sand collapses like a wet sand castle. If the crab were to be trapped outside his burrow by the rising water, he would be in serious danger of forming the first course of a fish's dinner.

As the time for high tide draws closer, the *U. pugilator* visits his burrow more and more often until he finally feels the bottom of his house getting wet from the water rising through the sand. Then he quickly sets to work pulling sand into the burrow with the legs on one side of his body and packing it into a plug. The holes are not very deep. The job is usually not completed long before the water reaches the level of the burrow. The water continues to rise in the sand, and the bottom of the hole collapses. Simultaneously, the water flows over the top of the burrow and fills the spaces between the sand grains of the plug. Once there is water between the grains, the air still in the burrow is trapped, for it cannot push the water aside to get through the tiny spaces. This trapped air holds up the walls of the burrow as well and the crab finds himself in a little air-filled cavern beneath the surface, safe from predators who are cruising the water above him for food.

The *Uca pugnax* completely lack this instinct to protect themselves by closing their hole before the water rises. In the muds where they normally live, the walls of their burrows are cohesive enough not to collapse. They have no need for the behavior pattern their relatives have developed. The water doesn't enter their burrows until it pours into the entrance which remains open throughout high tide. *Uca pugnax* can go home anytime and find home still there. They usually wait until the water is up to their knees before retiring. Perhaps this explains why they are not found living on the creek banks. Any individual who tries to change his habitat gets trapped at the surface of the rising tide and is promptly eaten.

The rising tide can be a time of disaster for marsh animals, especially those unusually high tides that result from onshore winds piling already high tides higher still. The marsh wrens' nests are built in the tallest *Spartina* along the edges of the creeks. During some spring tides, the water rises high enough to flood the nests. When this happens, the eggs or young die within a few minutes. The same fate can overtake rice rats who have evicted the wrens or use a male nest as home. In both cases, success of nesting rests on getting started just after one spring tide and finishing before the next so that, when the dangerous waters rise, the young are old enough to escape.

The rails often have their nests flooded, but their eggs can survive a dunking in seawater. The young have no problem. They are able to run about as soon as they dry off after hatching. They can float and swim on the rising waters, staying in the tall grasses hidden from predators on the prowl for helpless animals.

In midsummer, the effect of an especially high tide on the insects is spectacular. The insects crawl up the plants to escape the rising waters. But, as the water rises higher and higher, more and more of the plants are completely submerged. The animals hop, jump, and fly onto other plants that protrude still higher above the water. A few individuals can be found riding on the surface tension of the water. The marsh disappears beneath a mirror of blue reflecting the sky. Only the tallest grasses along the creeks mark the meandering channels and these grasses are weighted and bending at the tips, alive with insects.

Sparrows and wrens from the marsh, buntings, and warblers from the land, gulls and terns from the beach, and swallows, dip, fly, settle, and swim along the twisting lanes of helpless insects and gorge themselves. Some of the larger insects crawl down the stems of the *Spartina* or dive under the surface of the water to escape the ravaging birds.

At more normal midsummer high waters, the marsh is a much calmer place. The ants living in the *Spartina* stems block the entrance to their nests and remain snug and dry inside their hollow, growing houses. Large fish, gray-green monsters lighted by murky sunlight, drift slowly up the larger creeks looking for food, usually smaller fish, minnows, menhaden, and bass. These small fish school up the creeks, trying to avoid the hunters.

Raccoons out on the marsh, which are varying their land diet with marsh crabs and shellfish, build a nest by pulling *Spartina* stalks together along the side of a creek into a half floating, half supported platform on which they stay dry until the falling tide exposes the supper table.

Insects crawl up the plant stalks ahead of the water or fly away to the land, attempting to avoid the cruising dragonflies and swallows as they go.

Sesarma cinereum, the square-backed crab, climbs

Sleeping raccoon

grass stalks also, but more heavily and clumsily than the insects. The crabs frequently fall off, but as they live only in either dense *Spartina* stands where the stems are thick and strong, or near land where they can leave the marsh altogether to stay above water, their plight is not overwhelming. The other, or purple square-backed crab, *Sesarma reticulatum,* hides in the mud at both high and low water. It makes a specialty of feeding at mid-tide when it has the area more or less to itself. The animals active in air are going into hiding and those active underwater have not yet come out when *S. reticulatum* emerges to feed on *Spartina* leaves.

The snails, both *Littorina* and *Melampus*, climb out of the water at high tide. They may cluster above the stems of the plants in areas of sparse and stunted *Spartina* until they are piled one atop the other at the base and up on the stems to the limit of available space.

Rising tide signals not retirement and rest but the setting of the table for other marsh animals. Mud crabs, *Panopeus herbstii,* the size of fiddler crabs, and the larger *Eurytium limosum*, come out of their holes and wander about between the grass stems looking for almost anything edible. They will devour all sorts of animals, dead or alive, just so they are small or inactive enough to be handled. Some of the smallest aquatic animals get up into the grass, little fish an inch or so long and tiny squid recently hatched from their finger-shaped egg cases. They look for prey, safe for the moment from larger predators which would make a meal of them. Some will fail to escape with the ebbing water and will fall victim to exposure or to the first marsh animal which comes upon them.

During a normal high tide, birds living on the marsh hunt for food. The long-billed marsh wren, seaside and sharp-tail sparrows, laughing gulls, and redwings look for the tender insects which serve as concentrated sources of the protein necessary for the rapid growth of the young birds. Like the other marsh young, they must grow up quickly to be ready to take care of themselves by the time winter approaches.

Porpoises may come up the creeks at high water and sport about in the mud between the streamside *Spartina* stalks while they eat clams and crabs. They make a great racket in the air with their splashing and whooshing breathing, and in the water with the squeals and clicks by which they talk and find their way about.

In the south, an occasional alligator may swim into the grass looking for a snack, perhaps a diamond-backed terrapin which is looking for a snack of snails.

At the opposite end of the size range, inch-long sand shrimp swim up into the flooding waters and allow themselves to be carried into the marsh. They become silent, ghostly little armored hunters looking for a recently dead crab, the unprotected end of a worm that has failed to make it inside the burrow, or the unwary larvae of some crustacean relative. The sand shrimp flood and ebb with the tide, staying always in the water. Like fish, they visit the marsh only because the water does, but, as the marsh is a marsh only because seawater visits it, they are part of it.

The summer wears on. The baby crabs, hatched from the red-orange egg masses hung under their mothers, have drifted with the tides, eaten, or been eaten. Those that have survived return to the marsh as tiny crabs to replace the adults that have fallen victim to rails, raccoons, herons, and other crab eaters.

Late summer and autumn rains combine with the high tides to wet the highest areas of the marsh more frequently than they did in summer. During the alternating wetting and drying, the salt marsh mosquito, *Aedes sollicitans,* becomes more abundant than at any other time of year. Their eggs, laid on the damp mud, begin to develop at once. At summer temperatures, the larvae are ready to hatch in less than two days, although the hatching may take more than a week at colder times of year. Once the larvae are ready, they need the special stimulus of getting wet before they will hatch. Eggs can live very nicely on damp mud, on which larvae would die. The females spread eggs all over the surface of the damp mud where they develop and wait for a puddle to form.

When submerged by rain or an extra high tide, the eggs hatch within minutes. In warm weather they will grow into adults in less than a week. It is an excellent system for taking maximum advantage of temporary pools. The females couldn't possibly get to the pools and lay eggs in all of them. The delay in hatching and the ability of the eggs to live for weeks and even months in the mud assures that each pool will be full of wrigglers from almost the moment it forms. In such a humid environment as the marsh, it is a rare pool that dries up before it can produce at least a few mosquitoes. If it does, there are always a few eggs that didn't hatch on the first flooding that will take advantage of the next.

The grasses slow their growth of leaves and begin to elongate the stalk that will raise the flowers and seeds up into the air. The baby birds are now grown and are chasing their own insects or catching their own crabs.

The insects reach the egg-laying state, the pupal stage, or the adult stage, depending on whether they will try to survive the winter as eggs resting in the mud, as dormant pupae in plants, or as adults hiding in a crack or under the soil.

All the organisms make their preparations for the slowing of activities that is to follow. They do not know what is to follow, nor can they make plans for the future. They simply feel that the days are growing shorter and the nights cooler. They respond automatically with the built-in system that has assured the survival of their species through countless winters.

At the end of summer and in early autumn, the water may blaze with light on dark nights. This light is produced by a multitude of animals of various sorts that, like the fireflies, can illuminate themselves. Most of the light comes from single-celled microscopic dinoflagellates called, appropriately, *Noctiluca,* "light of the night." Sometimes the light comes from the nearly transparent comb jellies, *Ctenophores,* which use bioluminescence to light up the rows of ciliated "combs" with which they swim.

In general, none of these shallow-water organisms light up unless disturbed, unlike the many deep sea luminescent forms which light up of their own volition. It is not at all clear why the forms you see in the marsh creeks should produce light at all. It does not give them any obvious advantage over their dark neighbors.

Regardless of what it does for the producers of the light the luminescence provides a spectacular show for anyone fortunate enough to be able to wade, swim, or float through the marsh creeks on one of the illuminated dark nights. Every disturbance of the water produces bright sparks outlining the disturbing objects. The wader can see the outline of his legs and feet moving through the water. The boater sees the outline of his boat and its wake. If there are schools of fish in the water, they become streaks of light as they dart away.

Autumn starts in the north and moves south during September and October. The grasses mature their seed heads. Some of the more adventurous aquatic animals of the marsh, worms, and mud crabs turn toward the sea where the water never goes below freezing below its surface.

The birds fly south. The swallows start almost before summer is over. They hawk their way over the ribbon of marshes, feeding on insect swarms as they move along.

The seed eaters follow the ripening grasses southward. The ducks, including many that were raised inland, congregate on the marshes where they can move up on the high tides to the ponds filled with widgeon grass or the concentration of snails near the land. They feed with relative safety while the hiding places in the marsh are filled with water. When the tide recedes, every creek bank provides cover for human hunters, who, during the season, try to take a share of the productivity of the marsh.

The rails with their young migrate south, hiding their ungainly flight at night. They are also taken by the hunters who wait for the extra high storm tides of fall to concentrate the secretive birds in the smallest amount of cover, the clumps of grasses remaining above even the highest tides. Autumn is also the season when in some parts of Massachusetts and New Jersey men invade the marsh with mowers to cut and gather the marsh hay from the flats for use as garden mulch. It is ideal for this as it contains no weeds to shed seeds which could contaminate the garden. The grass is also used for packing material as it is tough and springy.

Autumn is the time when mink with fine winter coats come silently along the creeks to fish for succulent clam dinners. The young mink are on their own now and join the number of fierce mink predators stalking the marshes. In freshwater areas, mink are the terror of muskrats whose flesh they delight in. On the marshes, clams and crabs are the principal food available, although the mink are willing to vary their diet with a rice rat or an unwary bird whenever possible.

When the marsh creeks get colder than the offshore waters, the high tides are warmed by waters coming from offshore. The fish move out and leave the marshes for the winter. The schools of young menhaden gather into the shoals that will provide future seasons' catches and move into deeper water. Young bass seek to avoid the cold of the cooling shallows and follow the menhaden offshore. The little fish of the creeks similarly avoid the coldest waters, although none of them go far from the marsh. Silversides are no longer found in large numbers at the edges of the marsh. Sticklebacks go to the deeper creeks.

The blood of fishes freezes at a higher temperature than does seawater. Although wintering killifish increase the sugar in their blood, which acts as a kind of antifreeze, they will still freeze when seawater is still liquid. The fish are often supercooled, but not frozen, down in the mud at a slightly lower than freezing temperature. They can remain in this condition all winter as long as they don't touch ice. Once a part of their body contacts ice, they will freeze and die. Their muddy blanket keeps them unfrozen, but not warm.

The herons that fed on the small fish go south to eat where the fish are still abundant in shallow water.

The plants die down. The remaining marsh animals

burrow into the mud below the frost line and retreat toward the low water level. The living activities in the marsh slow and almost stop in the far north.

The noises of marsh life stop. Whistling winds, coldly lapping waves, and the grinding of ice across frozen mud take the place of rustling grass, calling birds, and buzzing insects.

Life in the marsh awaits spring.

11. Marsh Production

THE SALT MARSH IS A CONVENIENT SYSTEM IN WHICH
to study the workings of nature because the rigors of
the environment have put severe limits on the numbers
of kinds of organisms that can live there. The abundance of species that confuses the picture of a nearby
freshwater marsh or an upland grassland or a forest has
been reduced to a level that can be more easily managed. There are fewer kinds of plants living in the salt
marsh and there are fewer animals living on the plants.
Since the system is less complex, analysis is simplified.
Simplified, but not simple. The work of many biologists
over many years has gone into the analysis of the salt
marsh.

All of the marsh production begins with the capture
of light energy from the sun by plants. The plants which
come to mind first are the grasses and bordering plants,
the large ones that can be plucked and studied.

Algae living in the marshes are also very important
as producers. There are forms of algae that live on the
surface of the mud, migrating up and down to adjust
conditions of light and heat to their advantage, as the
tides cover and uncover their habitat. There are algae
living on the surface of the lower parts of *Spartina*
stalks or growing on any solid surface in the marsh that
is wet regularly by the tides.

There are floating algae that live in the water continually, entering the marsh at high tide and leaving again
at low. These, when they settle onto the surface of the

mud or are filtered out of the water by filter-feeding animals, also contribute to marsh production.

In the southernmost marshes, *Spartina* grows to some extent throughout the year, although most of the growth takes place during spring and summer. In the northern marshes, *Spartina* grows only during the warmer parts of the year. The algae in the northernmost to the southernmost marshes grow throughout the year.

In the southern marshes, the algae, diatoms, and flagellates living on the mud grow about as fast during winter as during summer. In winter, when the sun is weak, they grow on top of the mud during low tide where they are exposed to the full light of the sun. In summer, the sunlight is too strong at low tide and the algae hide in the mud. They come to the surface and grow during high tide when the water reduces the intensity of the midsummer sun.

In the New England marshes, the diatoms hide in the sand during high tide and at night and come to the surface only during low tide in the daylight. The more northern sunlight is not so strong that they must hide from it. They have an internal clock which tells them when to emerge for they will come out of the sand at the correct time even in constant light and temperature in a laboratory, away from any possible clue as to the time of high tide. They continue to match the tides for as long as ten days, even to the point of abandoning the evening time of low tide when it runs into the darkness and shifting their emergence to the low that comes the following morning.

The algae and the *Spartina* are the producers of food for the marsh. All of the animals, consumers, depend on the plants for food, either eating them directly or eating animals which in turn eat plants.

Spartina is eaten by grasshoppers which may be very abundant in the southern marshes. The grass is also eaten by one of the mud crabs, *Sesarma reticulatum,* which feeds on the outermost, oldest leaves of the plant. A number of bugs also feed directly on *Spartina.* Plant

Long-horned grasshopper

bugs, *Trigonotylus*, cinch bugs, *Ischnodemus*, the plant hoppers, *Prokelisia*, have sharp beaks like those of aphids with which they pierce the *Spartina* and suck its juices.

There are plant-eating beetles, ants which feed on *Spartina,* and flies which feed on the surface of the plants, some sponging up exudates from the grass. Nematodes feed on *Spartina* roots. The larvae of the most abundant marsh flies, the tiny grass flies, live within the stems eating plant tissue.

Many other animals feed directly on algae, but they also feed, simultaneously, on detrital particles of *Spartina*. Most of the grass is not eaten directly but dies from many causes: maturation of outer leaves, maturation of the whole aboveground part of the plant at seed formation, freezing, trampling by large animals, and washouts after heavy rains.

When it dies, the plant can no longer protect itself from the attacks of bacteria which immediately begin to decompose the grass. From a bacterium's point of view, it begins to eat the dead plant. From our view, the bacteria decompose the grass and change it to detritus. A bacterium is too small to have room inside itself to take food in and digest it. Digestion must be performed on the outside of the cell. This results in the food breaking up into smaller and smaller pieces as digestion continues. The result is that the bacterial food decomposes before your eyes. In the tidal waters of the salt marsh, the small particles with their associated bacteria, detritus, are carried by the water and spread about on the surface of the marsh. They then become available as a source of food for many animals which are not equipped to eat *Spartina* while it is still in big pieces.

Much of the original plant material is used by the bacteria during the process of changing dead *Spartina* into detritus. Bacteria are living things just like other salt marsh organisms and need energy to keep going.

The grasses consist largely of cellulose, the substance from which plants make their cell walls and which gives them their strength. Cellulose is highly resistant to digestion by most animals, but it is digested by many fungi and bacteria. As the *Spartina* is digested by these microorganisms on the marsh, more and more of the cellulose is converted into bacterial and fungal protoplasm, which is then easily digested by animals. The *Spartina* decays. Much of its substance is lost to the animals as a result of the bacterial metabolism, but the end-product mixture of broken plant parts and bacteria is a better food for the animals than the original grass.

In the process of decomposing, bits of *Spartina* may pass many times through the guts of detritus eaters. On each passage, the bacteria and any other digestible portions are used by the animal. The remainder passes on through the gut and is deposited on the marsh surface. Further bacterial action converts more of the cellulose into suitable food which may then be passed through another animal's digestive tract and the process repeated.

Spartina alterniflora growing along the creeks decays more quickly than *S. patens* growing near land. In the spring and far into the summer, last year's *S. patens* growth is still in place, a springy carpet beneath the current year's growth. As the tidal currents are not strong up in the higher parts of the marsh, having been slowed by the lower *S. alterniflora* marshes, *S. patens* is not washed away.

Since the dead high marsh grass does not wash away, it decomposes in place. Like a farmer's hay left too long in the field, much of the protein, carbohydrate, and fat left in the leaves oxidizes in place. When the grass finally falls to the ground, the bacterial process breaks it up. The grass and bacteria then become food for the animals living in that area of the marsh.

This detritus, with the algae with which it is always mixed as a result of tidal action, is the most abundant food on the marsh. Most of the animals living there make at least some use of it. At the small end of the size spectrum, there are protozoa and nematode worms which are minute enough to be selective in their feeding habits. They pick out individual bacteria or algae. Many other nematodes and all of the larger organisms cannot be so selective. They eat all portions of the detritus-bacteria-algae mixture.

Earthworm relatives which have learned to live in the salt mud eat their way through the surroundings like their terrestrial kin. Many nematodes which would seem to be small enough to be selective appear to feed indiscriminately on all parts of the mixture. The contents of the stomachs of these small animals can be seen through their bodies with the aid of a microscope.

Many kinds of larvae of marsh insects, mosquito larvae among them, and some adult flies, eat the detritus mixtures. The *Dolichopodid,* or long-legged flies, are usually predatory as adults, but the marsh species eat detritus.

This fact was discovered by an experiment made by a scientist from the University of Georgia who marked some detritus with radioisotopes. Animals eating the detritus were automatically marked by the isotopes. When these animals were eaten by predators, the predators became marked. The detritus eaters, including the *Dolichopodid* flies, began to pick up the marking immediately and were most heavily marked at the end of one week. The radioactivity in their bodies then declined as the isotope decayed and was diluted by subsequent feeding on unmarked food. The marking of predators was delayed for they could not pick up the isotope until their prey was marked. Predators required three to four weeks to reach their maximum isotope content. The different times required for various species to accumulate the isotope clearly distinguished predators from detritus feeders.

Fiddler crabs are well adapted to feeding on detritus. They scoop up a glob of sediment with their small claws, one-handedly in the males, two-handedly in the females. The material is continually fed into the mouth, which is not really a mouth but a series of six modified legs which cover the opening to the digestive tract.

These legs, aside from the outermost pair which functions as a cover for the others, are equipped with a set of bristles arranged on paddle-shaped leg segments. These are used to manipulate the potential food so that the larger particles are either crushed or separated from the fine material. Only the fine portion is swallowed. The larger portion gradually accumulates in the sorting chamber until it is spit neatly into a claw and put back on the marsh surface.

On looking closely at the mud or sand between the grass plants, you can see tiny scrape marks where the small claws have picked up food. Scattered among the scrape marks are lumps of rejected material and tiny, harder cylindrical feces, the remains of the crabs' dinner.

Snails feed on the surface of the mud as they crawl along, scraping it with their radulae, ribbons of teeth which resemble a miniature file. The teeth of the file point inward so that, when it is pulled back into the snail's mouth, it brings a sample of the substrate with it. Snails also accomplish a lot of their feeding by rasping off the algae growing on the surface of the lower parts of *Spartina* stalks along with the detritus that has settled there.

The largest detritus feeders are mullet and menhaden. These fish come up into the marsh creeks and eat the detritus directly, either by filtering it out of the water or by swallowing the bottom mud.

All of the filter-feeding animals living in the marsh eat the detritus-algae soup. The word "soup" is most appropriate in this case since these feeders get their food by straining it from water. The soup includes material stirred up from the bottom by the activities of the feeders as well as that already floating, so the filter feeders have a hand in preparing their soup. Marsh mussels are the most conspicuous member of this group.

Mussels begin to filter as soon as the tide wets them when the surface of the shells may still be almost entirely above water. The particles of food in the water are caught on a mesh of mucus threads secreted over the bivalves' gills and moved to the mouth by special bands of cilia. Before swallowing, the material is sorted by size. The smaller particles are selected. The larger particles are rejected as pseudofeces which accumulate around the mussels when they are periodically forced from the shell.

Other filter feeders include the oysters at the edges of the marshes and in the shallow creeks, clams in the pools and lower parts of newly forming marshes, and some polychaete annelids. These most common of the annelids are tiny animals, only a fraction of an inch long, and are widely distributed throughout the marshes.

There are few large animals that feed directly on the living grass or on dead grass before it is broken up. Most of the herbivores of the salt marsh feed on *Spartina* only after it has been broken down into detritus. The tides are partly responsible for this situation. The ground is too soft to support the weight of large grazing animals and the marshes are too strung out in space and have too rigorous a climate to have developed a special grazing fauna of their own.

On the savannahs and prairies of the world, most of the grass is directly eaten by large herbivores, bison, antelope, and cattle, while it is green and growing. The salt marsh grassland is more like a mature temperate forest in which the leaves and trees generally die and are decomposed before they find their way into the stomachs of the animals that live there.

A detritus-feeding community is different from a grazing one in several important ways. The plant-eating animals tend to be small rather than large and the largest animals are carnivores rather than herbivores. The food, because of the time required for decay, is evened out. While the salt marsh grasshoppers find a good supply of tender leaves during only a few months of the year, the detritus eaters have a constant supply. The decaying process is slowed during the cold months but at this time the needs of the animals are slowed too. There is a renewed burst of decay of last year's crop in the warm spring, which coincides with most of the animals' growth.

Carnivorous animals make their living and get their energy by eating all of these plant eaters. The predators are not as handily divided into separate groups as are the herbivores. They are usually willing to eat anyone they come across as long as the potential prey is small or weak enough to be overpowered. Certain of the predators are especially adapted for eating insects. Since insects include most of the animals that feed directly on the living *Spartina,* the insect eaters are only one step away from the plants, and two steps away from the life-giving sun.

The most important insect predators are the spiders. There are hunting spiders which include the wolf spiders that rush their prey, running crab spiders, and jumping spiders. None of these have a fixed place of abode but are nomad over the marsh.

There are web-weaving spiders and stick spiders whose elongated bodies, presumably, give them some protection from bird predators while they wait by their webs for some unfortunate insect to blunder along.

Some of the insects of the salt marsh are fierce eaters of other insects. The larvae of the greenhead flies are as fierce to any small animals they meet in the mud as the adult females are to any of their prey. The larvae are maggots, soft, elongate, leathery-skinned, lumpy individuals with a pair of organs for breathing air at one end and a pair of sharp jaws at the other. They wriggle through the mud eating anything they come across, including others of their kind. If a number of *Tabanus* maggots are put together in a dish, the end result is one fat, temporarily contented individual.

There are larvae of the *Sciomyzid* flies, small flies

without common names found widely on the marsh although not common anywhere, whose larvae, as far as is known, feed on snails. Although it is not a certainty, this group probably attacks the marsh snails, *Littorina* and *Melampus*.

Among adult insects, there are beetles, which feed on injured and sluggish insects, predatory bugs, which capture and suck their prey dry, and robber flies and dragonflies, which capture their prey on the wing. The robber flies, among the most formidable, sometimes even swoop down on and eat grasshoppers.

Finally, there are the parasitic wasps which live as larvae within one insect host. By the end of larval growth, when they are ready to pupate and turn into adult wasps, they have ungraciously killed their host by eating him from the inside. They are like parasites in that they live within their prey and like predators in that they kill it. They are often quite specific as to what species of insect they will attack and, because of this specialization, have been used to control insect pests.

In this marsh food web, birds and mammals can make life hazardous for the insects. Wrens, sparrows, redwings, swallows, willets, gulls, and rails eat considerable quantities of insects. They harvest them, also, to feed their young which are raised on or near the marsh.

The larger mammals, raccoons and mink, eat the

Raccoons fishing

detritus-algae eaters rather than insects. Mussels, clams, and fiddler crabs, being larger as adults than insects, are more attractive food items for these larger animals. The bigger birds, clapper rails, ducks, and shorebirds, also eat more crabs and snails than insects for the same reason.

Most of the aquatic animals that invade the marsh at high tide eat crabs, snails, and worms more often than insects. The insects avoid being caught underwater where fish and predatory crabs find them easy game.

At the apex of the web of relationships that defines the eating habits of the marsh dwellers are the top predators. The marsh hawk or harrier cruises up and down the marsh looking for mice and small birds. Short-eared owls follow the same pattern, often flying during the day as well as at night. Bitterns catch fish, shrimp, and mice by alternately stalking along in the shallows and then freezing motionless as the prey approaches. Ospreys hunt for fish that come in with the tides to eat smaller fish. Eagles wait for the osprey to make a good catch and then steal the fish. Porpoises take clams and crabs on the edges of the marsh. Large

Marsh hawk

predatory fish, like most of the sport fish, come in to feed. Finally, man is at the pinnacle. He hunts and fishes and often kills for pleasure many of the fish and fowl living on the marsh production far from its beginning in the photosynthesis of the *Spartina* and algae.

Production begins with the sunlight falling on the marsh plants. Some of the amounts of production in different parts of the marsh system have been worked out for the Georgia and Cape Cod marshes. We have based our understanding of salt marshes as sources of food for various animals, including ourselves, on these studies.

Only a part of the energy that reaches the plants as sunlight can be used. The radiant heat wavelengths are not used at all. The plants use only the ends of the visible spectrum. Chlorophyll absorbs red and blue light only. The remainder, which looks green, is reflected or passes on through the plants, giving them their characteristic color.

Marsh plants manage to capture only about six percent of the sun's energy reaching the surface of the marsh during the year. This six percent figure was found for the southern marshes where there is some plant growth throughout the year. In the more northern marshes, where *Spartina* production stops completely during the winter and only the algae are active, the figure is not as high, although they are probably as efficient producers in summer as the southern marshes.

The marsh plants use some of this captured energy for their life processes. *Spartina* is a high user, consuming about half of the energy it captures. The algae are super-manufacturers. They use only about ten percent of what they produce, leaving in their substance a large reservoir of available energy for plant-eating animals.

Marsh plants catch only six percent of the available sunlight falling on the marsh, but there are few natural or man-made systems that do as well. A cornfield at its height of growth manages to capture only two percent of the energy of sunlight. A coral reef can capture only

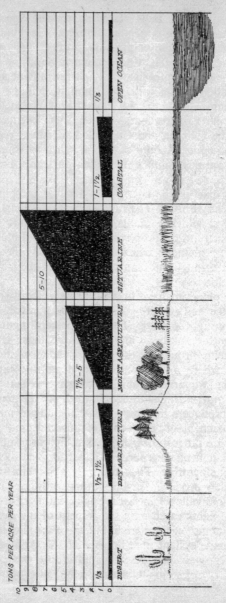

Comparative production rates

about three percent. By comparison, the salt marsh is a very productive spot in nature.

If production were to be expressed in weight, you would find that, on the average, the salt marsh produces nearly ten tons of organic matter on every acre in a year. By comparison, an average yield of wheat is about one and one half tons per acre per year, including stems and leaves. The best hay lands in this country produce about four tons per acre per year and the best wheat yields in the world exist in northern Europe where, with great effort, the farmers are able to coax seven tons per acre per year from the land. By sheer tonnage, a marsh is a luxuriant producer.

In the ocean, the yield of coastal waters offshore, but still within the limits of the continental shelf, is from one to one and one half tons per acre per year. The open oceans produce only one third of this amount.

Estuaries in general and salt marshes in particular are unusually productive places. None of the common agriculture, except possibly rice and sugarcane production, comes close to producing as much potential animal food as do the salt marshes. The agricultural crops which approach this high figure are fertilized and cultivated at great expense. The marsh is fertilized and cultivated only by the tides.

Marshes are productive for several reasons, all of which are a result of the meeting of land and sea. The tides continually mix the waters and, by their rise and fall, water the plants. Harmful accumulations of waste products, are diluted and removed. Nutrients are brought in continuous supply. The plants can put energy into growth which in another environment they might have to use for collecting nutrients. The meeting of fresh and salt waters tends to trap nutrients in the regions of such meeting and this concentration of nutrients promotes plant growth. The materials coming down the rivers tend to flocculate and settle out when they reach the increasingly salty estuarine waters. But the settled materials are not lost. *Spartina* roots use them. The tides continually stir the settled material and make the nutrients available for use by the phytoplankton.

Clams, oysters, and mussels help form the sediment and nutrient trap because of their method of feeding. They remove all of the particles from a large volume of water as it passes over their gills and deposit most of them in neat pseudofeces bundles.

Although marshes concentrate the nutrients, they do not create them. They must also be brought in from someplace. Some of the necessary nitrate is actually extracted from the air by way of nitrogen-fixing blue-green algae that live on the marsh mud. Other nutrients come into the marsh with the water, either from the rivers or from the sea. A considerable amount comes with the soil that washes into the marshes from the land.

Nutrient concentrations in soils are thousands of times greater than those in waters. As a result, plants growing in soils are more productive than those floating in the water. A relatively small amount of soil can bring a large amount of plant nutrients into the marsh. It may even be deposited on just a few days of the year when the river carries an extra heavy burden of sediment resulting from an occasional flooding rain far from the marsh.

Another reason for high marsh productivity is the quick rate of turnover of nutrients. These essential compounds are not locked up in organic structures that stand or lie in the marsh for years before they decompose and release the nutrients for reuse. The algae replace themselves in a matter of days and the abundant bacteria of the marsh in a matter of hours. Even the *Spartina*, which uses a large amount of nutrients to produce its stems and leaves, dies within half a year after any part of the plant appears.

There is some accumulation of undecomposed plant parts in the form of peat, especially in the more northern marshes, but the amount that accumulates is a minute fraction of the total production. Because the marsh is such an active community, nutrients become available about as fast as they are needed and limitation of plant growth by nutrient deficiency is not as important on salt marshes as it is in a typical marine or terrestrial situation.

Finally, the marshes are productive because there is almost no time during the year, even in the north, when there is not some plant growth taking place. In the south, it is warm enough for the *Spartina* to grow all year. At the latitudes of the mangroves, all plants grow all of the time if they are well watered. But in the north, where the land plants and *Spartina* cease activity during the winter, the algae in the marshes continue to grow throughout the year. The relatively constant growth of the mud algae in southern marshes and the midwinter blooming of the algae in the waters of the northern marshes are examples of year-round photosynthetic activity which helps move the marshes ahead of their neighboring terrestrial or marine areas in production.

Of the bounteous ten tons of possible food per marsh acre, the insects feeding directly on the *Spartina* use only a small part, less than four tenths of a ton. Most of the *Spartina* is left to die and be decomposed by bacteria.

As a result of the bacterial activity there are about five tons of suitable detritus-algae food available every year from each acre of marsh. The detritus-algae eaters eat about one-ninth of this food. Both groups of animals, the plant eaters and the detritus-algae eaters, use up most of the energy they get from their food and put the rest into the building of their bodies. The carnivores live on these animals, consuming about one hundred and fifty pounds, eighty percent of which they change into heat during the course of their activities while the other twenty percent is built into the protoplasms of their bodies. These numbers resulted from studies of the marshes in Georgia and are the only such numbers that exist at present.

The marsh plants are the most important consumers of the energy they capture from the sunlight. Bacteria are the next most important group and consume about one seventh as much as the plants. Moving down, animals are only about one seventh as important as the bacteria. When all this consumption is added together, however, we have accounted for only fifty-five percent of the energy that remained after we allowed for use by plants. Four and a half tons dry weight per acre of marsh production is left over.

The tide giveth and the tide taketh away. It is the tide that makes the high production possible and then removes half of it before animals of the marsh get a chance to use it. But what is denied the animals of the marsh is given to the abundant animal life in the estuarine waters around the marsh.

On the high marsh, the excess production is probably transported not by the tides as detritus but by the animals. Animals eat detritus and move about. Insects walk and fly and are eaten by predatory insects and birds, which move about even more. *Melampus* feeds on algal-detritus and in turn furnishes food for the black ducks which spend much of their time on estuarine waters.

The tides continually wash a part of the marsh production into the creeks and bays where fish, shrimp, and oysters lie in wait. Without the marsh, these animals could not survive in the numbers which are characteristic of the southern estuaries. Because the area of salt marsh along the southern coast is about twice as great as the area of open water, the marsh detritus washed out into the water can support about twice as much animal life in the estuaries as is found in the marsh itself!

PART III

Marsh Conservation

12. The Indispensable Marshes

THE MARSH-ESTUARINE SYSTEM SUPPORTS A LARGE number of economically important species of fish and shellfish. The fish and shellfish can be grouped together depending on the stage in their life histories at which they make use of the estuaries. Some live in and spawn in the sea as adults, but the young come into the shallow, productive waters to mature. In this group are mullet, menhaden, and most of the commercially valuable shrimp. Other species come into the estuaries to spawn, an example of which is the sea trout or weakfish. The adults of this group of fish may move north and south along the coast for considerable distances, but they or their larvae need merely to turn westward to get to the estuaries and marshes so essential for the young growing stages.

Still other species spend their life in the sea but pass through the estuaries on their way to freshwater areas where they spawn. The adults of striped bass, shad, and alewife return immediately to the sea after spawning, but the young linger behind to develop and grow, first in freshwater and then in the partly salty estuaries.

Some fish that live as adults at sea during the colder times of year come inshore during summer to feed in the productive estuarine region, as do summer flounder, winter flounder, scup, and bluefish. Some of the winter flounder spawn inshore as well.

There is another group of species that live their entire life within the marsh-estuarine system. Important in

Estuarine fishes: shad; alewife; striped bass

this group are the shellfish: oysters, clams, and crabs. A few fish also stay throughout the year, especially along the southern portion of the coast where the shallow waters remain quite warm all winter. The sea trout, which moves out to sea during winter in the north, remains in the estuaries in the south.

There are many kinds of small fish that live within the marsh and estuaries. Species of minnows find these shallow waters ideal places to live and grow. These little fish become food for many of the larger, commercially valuable fish just mentioned. They are also important food items for many of the birds that live on or feed in the marsh.

Not only are individual marshes important, but from the pattern of movements made by many animals, it is obvious that the whole complex of coastal marshes is important. Marshes and their associated estuaries have existed all along the coast for thousands of years. Fish and birds have evolved depending on finding marshes *all* along the coast, wherever they wander. The preservation of a few marshes, here and there, will not serve for their existence.

Two thirds of the value of the commercial catch of fish and shellfish landed on the East Coast of the

United States comes from species that live at least part of their life cycle in the marsh-estuaries. A little less than one half of the Pacific coast fisheries comes from species that spend at least a part of their life in the rather meager marsh-estuarine system that exists there. It is estimated by fishery experts that eighty to ninety percent of the fish gathered for market throughout the world come from shallow coastal waters.

Only tuna, haddock, yellowtail flounder, and ocean perch, among the twelve most important kinds of fish and shellfish taken in the United States, by either weight landed or value of the catch, are not associated with estuarine waters. Of these, only the tuna are open ocean fish. The others live in coastal waters.

The leading commercial fish, by weight landed, is menhaden, used in making fish meal and fertilizer. Menhaden depends heavily on estuaries and marshes in its young stages as does the most valuable commercial catch of all, shrimp.

The dependence of the commercial fisheries upon the shallow waters at the edge of the land is related to the productivity of various areas of the oceans. The estuaries and marshes are about ten times as productive as

Estuarine fishes: weakfish; mullet; menhaden

the coastal waters, which in turn are about ten times as productive as the open ocean waters.

In the open ocean, the plants are very small, floating phytoplankton, too little to be eaten by any but the smallest animals, zooplankton, also floating in the water. Zooplankters, in turn, are eaten by small fish, which are eaten by squids, which are eaten by large fish (such as tuna), which are eaten by man. The steps between open ocean plants and man may not always be as outlined, but the progression may include as many or more steps.

A comparable land situation on the grasslands would be that man would eat only cougars, which fed only on wolves, which fed only on cattle, which ate only grass. Even in the days when the plains were covered with bison and the wolves had not been killed off, a predator which fed only on wolves would have been able to furnish food for very few people.

We are confronted with the problem that, in the sea, we cannot use the animals that eat the plants. They are too small and too widely scattered to be economically caught. They contain too much indigestible matter for man to eat them in quantity, even if they could be economically caught. We must depend upon other animals to concentrate them into large, edible bodies before they are suitable for our use. Therein lies the value of the plankton-eating whales, which men are pushing toward extinction. Even they eat only animal plankton and are, therefore, comparable to the wolves rather than the cattle.

Only two groups of fish in the oceans can be compared to the cattle in feeding directly upon plants. One group is the fish, such as anchovies, that live in areas of constant high productivity next to the western edges of continents. Upwelling deep water here brings nutrients to the surface. Phytoplankton, larger than is typical of the ocean, grows abundantly and the anchovy feed directly upon the plants. The world's largest fishery, the anchovy fishery of Peru, depends on this combination of circumstances.

The other group of plant-eating fish includes mullet, menhaden and such non-fish fishery animals as shrimps and oysters. These animals live mostly on the constant supply of detritus from higher plants, including *Spartina,* as well as mangrove, eelgrass, and turtle grass which grow in shallow waters near salt marshes.

Unless we destroy them, our most valuable fisheries will always be those associated with the marshes and estuaries. We are up against too great a problem in gathering food from the open ocean beyond the shelf to make it successful. We may, someday, get more of the smaller fish from the open ocean, but only at an enormously greater cost.

Parts of marshes and associated estuaries could be logically used for aquiculture. Experiments at the Bears Bluff Laboratory in South Carolina, under the direction of Dr. Lunz, have shown that marsh ponds can produce two hundred fifty to four hundred pounds of fish per acre per year, one hundred pounds of crabs, and from three hundred to four hundred pounds of shrimp. This bounty was harvested without any effort at cultivation, except for predator control in the case of the shrimp. Considerably better yields could presumably be achieved with intensive culture. The upper limits are probably represented by fish and shrimp ponds in the Far East, where over one thousand pounds of shrimp and two thousand pounds of fish are produced on each acre of pond every year.

The animals suitable for pond culture include mullet, shrimp, crabs, and oysters, which can feed directly on detritus and algae. All of these animals eat the accumulation on the bottom of the pond. Their culture could be encouraged in shallow ponds covered with grass and having a soft bottom of organic and inorganic material on which algae could grow. Cultivation would be desirable to disrupt the mud-dwelling organisms which would otherwise consume a large amount of the production. The mud organisms form an intermediate step in the food chain leading to the desired animals, but their presence is not necessary and only detracts from the production of the desired end product.

Large areas of black rush marsh along the southeast coast might well be used for aquicultural research and eventually for commercial production. Perhaps the trapping of dredging spoils and the construction of ponds could be combined. Dredging spoils usually provide an ideal soft bottom. The use of dredging spoils for the creation of suitable shrimp bottom on otherwise hard bottoms has also been suggested by Dr. Lunz.

The sports fishery depends upon the coastal estuaries even more than does the commercial fishery, and much more money is involved in the sports industry. In 1965, the commercial fishery dependent upon estuaries brought nearly thirty million dollars to fishermen and more than seventy-five million to the industry as a whole. In that year, four million sports fishermen spent about four hundred million dollars on all aspects of their sport.

The two figures are not strictly comparable since the money spent by sports fishermen includes payment of hotel bills, costs of meals, and other such expenses, only indirectly related to the catching of fish. Still, the numbers illustrate the amount of money involved and the importance of the fish to those who spend that amount in trying to catch them and to those who provide the fishermen with food, lodging, and equipment. It is probable that most of the people involved have little idea of the importance of marshes to their sport or to their livelihood.

A similar argument holds for game and hunters. Salt marshes furnish homes for swamp rabbits, mink, muskrats, otters, and raccoons. They furnish homes and resting places for many waterfowl, especially along the northeast coast. Farther south the ducks tend to desert the coast for inland sites but their place for the hunters is taken by the marsh hen or clapper rail and to a lesser extent by other rails, gallinules, and snipe. Even pheasants use the *Spartina patens* marshes regularly in some areas.

All of these animals attract people to the marshes and their environs. These people hunt and trap the animals, getting satisfaction as well as meat for their efforts, and they leave a considerable sum of money in the hands of the local populations.

The number of people who take advantage of the shore area is immense. Just how many is difficult to know, but thirty-five percent of the population of the United States lives within one hundred fifty miles of the East Coast. Many people come to the shore at least once a year, and many come several times. In one way or another, a vast number of people have an interest in salt marsh preservation, or should have.

It is easier to study the adaptations of organisms in environments where they must be highly developed. The extreme changes in the salt marsh force the organisms living there to put forth their best efforts. If we wish, for example, to study the adaptations of plants to saline soils, it makes good sense to choose as subjects plants which have adapted to salt marshes. Not only do they live in salty soils but they must withstand periods of freshwater as well. A salt adaption mechanism which can be turned on and off will often be more easily made to give up its secrets than one which works steadily at one rate.

There is good evidence that variety is essential to the health of nature. We are all familiar with the idea that farmers find it necessary to spray their crops. They poison insects that attack domestic animals. They poison insects that eat crops. They protect crops against various types of devastating fungi. One of the principal reasons that this has come about is that farmers have taken variety out of the landscape.

Instead of a mixture of plants and animals in a field, there is only one kind of crop plant. Rather than a mixed group of animals spread over a wide area, there is a local congregation of just one type. When an enemy of a plant or animal finds its prey or its host, it literally finds a bonanza. A weasel in nature would never encounter the congregation of prey it finds in a hen house. Primitive farmers, whose hens roost in trees, have little to fear from the weasel. A modern farmer who simplifies nature to the point of having only chickens in a building would be ruined by a few weasel visits.

Ecologists have found that preserving variety in nature, even in just allowing roadsides and fencerows to go wild, can often reduce the problem of pests on crops. The wild areas, next to the fields, furnish homes for predators and parasites of crop pests. The predators and parasites have a short hop or flight to their prey or host. We don't yet know the details of most such interactions even on land, much less underwater. But the marshes provide valuable variety in our shallow water coastal regions.

There is yet another aspect of variety that is important. The salt marsh community of organisms is simple in comparison to those found in other environments. The marsh, within itself, is marked by a lack of variety, in spite of the fact that it lends variety to the larger scene. Few plants and animals have adjusted to the rigorous conditions of the salt marsh. The result is that the natural system found there bears a strong resemblance to the artificial, simple systems found in agriculture. But, unlike agriculture, the natural system is free of devastating pests. The harshness of the environment, which produced the simple marsh system, also keeps pests down.

There is certainly an economic incentive for preserving as much of the variety in nature as possible. The number of plants and animals that have been domesticated is very limited. Of some three hundred thousand species of plants in the world, only about three thousand are used. Many kinds are not used because they are poisonous, unpalatable, indigestible, unsuited to agricultural methods, or have little nutritive value. But many are simply untried, at least in modern civilization. It is an advantage to preserve as large a reservoir of untried plants as possible. Needs of the future that we cannot foresee may be satisfied by plants that we now overlook.

One such need is now developing in areas where land is irrigated. Irrigation is practiced in regions where there is little water and evaporation is rapid. If the water for irrigation is limited, as it usually is, there is great temptation to use only as much as is necessary to grow crops and no more. The water flows into the fields where it evaporates both from plants and directly from the soil. The salts in the water, originally not very concentrated, gradually become more concentrated by evaporation. If there is a large supply of water available and good drainage, flooding the fields will wash the salts away and no damage will be done. If the fields are not flooded, salts may accumulate until crops can no longer be grown.

These saline soils might be used to grow *Spartina* for cattle feed. Agricultural experts have probably thought of this, but we know of no place where the idea has been pursued. *Spartina* seeds germinate best in relatively low salinity, but once established will tolerate salinities which crop plants cannot withstand.

Rice is considered quite salt resistant among crops. It will grow in water containing about one part salt in one thousand parts of water. *Spartina* regularly grows in seawater which contains over thirty times that amount. Perhaps the *Spartinas*, as they now exist, are not entirely suitable for agriculture on inland saline soils, but might have to be improved by selective propagation. It might be well worth the effort. For three hundred years, cattle were fed on *Spartina* that grew naturally on salt marshes. Perhaps, with time, cattle will again be fed on *Spartina* from inland soils that have been ruined for other crops by improper irrigation.

There have been various tries at domesticating some

of the animals that live on the marsh. Clams have been artificially farmed in Massachusetts and attempts made to raise shrimp in South Carolina. Both efforts used pools in salt marsh areas. It is easier to grow shrimp food on marshes, making the tides do most of the work, than it is to grow it on other types of land, with man taking over the tidal role.

Shrimp, lobsters, clams, and oysters are the most valuable products we take from the sea. At the same time, they are the most amenable to management and farming. Clams and oysters do not move about in the water once they have passed through their larval stages. Initial efforts to farm the seas logically concentrate on these animals, for this success promises the greatest return for the effort. The salt marshes will be extremely valuable in domesticating marsh animals; that is, if they are still in existence when success is achieved.

Because the marshes lie along the edge of the sea, they are valuable in controlling floods that come from the sea. As they lie in front of the land, they take the brunt of blows delivered by storm waves. The water is quite shallow over the marshes, even during the highest storm tides. Shallow water makes waves break and as they break they expend the energy stored in them by storm winds. Breaking waves can cause enormous damage. They have been known to move solid breakwaters weighing over one thousand tons, to destroy small islands, and to throw rocks two hundred feet into the air.

Most of the damage caused by waves occurs where the waves first break. On a marsh, this is often where the bank rises from low tide level. Although pieces of it may be washed away, especially at the edge where the roots may not have firmly bound the mud together, or it may be partly covered with sand washed up by the storm and smothered, whatever happens, the marsh is a living thing. It can rebuild itself. The grasses can again grow out into the damaged area. New sediment can be trapped and bound into a firm substratum which further increases the growth of the grasses. The marsh can recover, become as it was, all without help or money cost.

But, if the marsh is destroyed, covered with dredging spoils and then with houses or industrial buildings, or converted into marinas, these structures can be damaged by waves. This involves a money cost because a building cannot repair itself.

After a severe storm, people all over the country are asked to contribute voluntarily or through taxes to aid those who suffered storm damage. We naturally help those who have been damaged by acts of nature. But it would be much less expensive to buy the marshes and preserve them than to allow development and pay the cost of damages that should never have occurred.

In the winter of 1953, a severe storm on the North Sea caused extensive damage along the coast of Lincolnshire, England. Beaches and shoreline structures were entirely washed away. But extensive salt marsh areas were little changed and what damage occurred was soon repaired by nature.

Many marshes are located where their value as protection for the shore is negligible. Wave damage never occurs there. But many marshes, standing between the land and low sandy barriers at the edge of the water, are important in absorbing wave damage. Most important as natural barriers for wave damage are the mangrove swamps.

In many places, mangroves grow directly on the edge of the sea. Hurricanes contribute some of the most severe wave damage that occurs in nature, and these are most common in tropical waters where mangroves live. Mangroves, as they are much taller than marsh grasses, offer greater resistance to wave passage. In fact, a well-developed mangrove swamp, though it cannot stop damage due to flooding, can completely stop the passage of waves.

The protective barriers of mangroves are often misused by land developers, especially on the Florida Keys. Often the developers' first act is to cut down all the mangroves. Then the low-lying ground is filled to bring it above sea level and houses built along the edge of the sea. They look beautiful along the sparkling, blue-green, quiet sea. But when the seas rise and tropical storms pass by, they are terrifyingly exposed.

The coral cays off the coast of British Honduras were originally formed of coral blocks and coral sands thrown up on the shallows by the sea. Once an islet was formed, it was invaded by vegetation which stabilized the sands. An important part of the vegetation was mangrove. These little islands were mapped and measured just before Hurricane Hattie struck the area in 1961 with two-hundred-mile-per-hour winds and seas fifteen feet above normal.

After the storm passed it was a simple matter to return to the cays and remap them to see what damage the storm had caused. The cays covered with their natural vegetation suffered little. The roots held the soil in place and the plants had slowed the waves so dramatically that, on the edges of these cays, there was actually an accumulation of five to seven feet of new material left by the storm. Other cays which had been cleared of natural vegetation and planted to coconuts did not fare so well. They suffered severe erosion. Trees were torn up and soil was washed away. Since an earlier survey in 1830 at least twenty of these cleared and farmed cays have disappeared completely, eaten away by tropical storms.

Salt marshes are valuable to us all. They are economically valuable in providing fish nursery grounds, protection from flood and storm damage, feeding grounds for birds, and sources of shellfish. They are aesthetically valuable as variety on our highly developed coastline.

As the only part of our shoreline that still looks much as it did when the first colonists landed, they are historically valuable. They are scientifically valuable both as places to study adaptations to a harsh environment and as some of the most productive natural areas known.

13. Pollution of Marshes

DUMPING OF SEWAGE, EITHER TREATED OR UNTREATED, takes its toll of marshes. Fish and shellfish which come from areas where there is untreated sewage pollution are not edible. It is usually assumed that exposure of polluted water to sunlight and air purifies it after a short time. To a degree this is true but biologists have recently discovered that fish coming from polluted water might act as a reservoir of infectious disease bacteria.

It is rare that completely untreated sewage is dumped directly into water. Only the smallest towns using such a system can continue it for any length of time. An intolerable situation quickly develops in sewage-infected water. However, dumping sewage that has received only primary treatment is not uncommon. In this treatment, solid wastes are filtered or allowed to settle out and the liquid remainder is channeled into the water. This liquid is rich in organic matter and may produce objectionable odors if not diluted with large quantities of water.

In other areas, sewage that has received secondary treatment, in which most of the dissolved organic matter is removed, usually in a trickling filter, may be put into estuaries. The outflow usually has only a small amount of dissolved organic matter, but it is rich in plant nutrients that were liberated as the organic matter was decomposed.

A small amount of raw sewage, aside from the problems of disease, is not necessarily a bad thing for an estuary. The sewage is oxidized in the water and grad-

Marsh destruction by a trash dump

ually releases its nutrients which then become available to plants. It is like fertilizing soil with manures. But if large amounts of raw sewage or large amounts of the rich organic effluent from a primary treatment plant are released into the water, the biochemical oxidation of the sewage may require more oxygen than is present in the water. The water becomes anaerobic, animals are killed, and in seawater where sulfates are plentiful, hydrogen sulfide is produced. The human nose is very sensitive to the smell of hydrogen sulfide, reminiscent of rotten eggs. By the time the odor has become apparent, damage has already been done. Many animals will have been killed by the absence of oxygen. Boston's old Black Bay became polluted, anaerobic, and finally so stinking that it had to be corrected and was filled in. Such a thing can still happen, especially in small marshes which have restricted circulation.

Effluent from secondary treatment is safe as far as disease or oxygen reduction is concerned. Its only effect is to fertilize the water. The fertilizer is immediately available to the plants and is not spread over a large area by gradual decomposition, as is the case with raw sewage. The phytoplankton and animals feeding on it grow abundantly. But it is possible to load the water with too much fertilizer and the estuary may become choked with phytoplankton. Growth can become so thick that light is shut off below the top layer. Algae, decomposing below the surface, may exhaust the oxygen in the water. Then the estuary reacts as if too much primary treatment effluent were released. In this case, no disease organisms may be involved. The Great Lakes are presently suffering from this type of pollution.

The easiest way to remove nutrients from the sewage treatment plant outflow is to dump the waste somewhere other than directly into water. Sewage effluent has been sprayed on fields or woodlands where the plants then remove most of the nutrients. This treatment requires large areas which can be sprayed and is expensive compared to dumping into a convenient creek or estuary. It is also possible to remove nutrients chemically. Usually the best safeguard for a healthy estuary is complete treatment of sewage and dumping of the effluent into streams where there is enough volume of water to dilute it to a safe level.

Most of the sewage that enters estuaries comes from towns and cities along the coast. Marinas are becoming an important source of raw sewage pollution. Each slip in a marina contains at least one boat. Each boat has at least one toilet, which may be used by a number of people on a weekend in summer. The toilets almost universally flush directly into the water in which the boat is floating.

Many small harbors along the coast have become so polluted that fish and shellfish cannot safely be taken from them. With the increasing popularity of boating, the problem is constantly growing. One solution might be to provide toilets on the marina dock connected to a proper sewage disposal system but even this would not prevent use of the shipboard facilities. A better solution would be to limit the size of marinas so that the offended body of water could be flushed by the tides without becoming polluted.

Garbage is another type of pollutant with which we are covering salt marshes. Beer cans, plastic cups and bottles are dumped into coastal waters in such numbers that in places they fairly stud drifts of trash at the high-water mark. There is probably no high-water mark in a marsh anywhere along the coast that does not contain at least one such memento of man's disregard for his environment. And of course, the many marshes that have been used for town dumps are completely smothered by garbage and trash.

This problem is constantly growing. Packaging of almost everything salable is getting more complex and indestructible. In 1940, citizens of the United Sates threw away about two pounds of garbage per person per day, making a grand total of fifty million tons a year. Twenty years later they threw out three and one half pounds a day, which added up to one hundred and fifteen million tons per year. This cannot be allowed to go on, and much could be done to reduce it simply by reducing unnecessary packaging—a solution not particularly attractive to the packaging industry. Alternative solutions would be to develop containers that decompose readily once used or return to the use of reusable containers.

For a time, detergents which came into the estuaries with sewage were an important pollutant. The detergents were not broken down by bacteria as were soaps and caused foaming, reduced oxygen penetration into the water, and poisoned aquatic animals. There was enough complaint from the general public that the detergent manufacturers changed detergent formulae. Detergents are now biodegradable and are no longer a serious problem. These pollutants gained notoriety because they formed a highly visible and bothersome foam. Other pollutants, not so highly visible, take much longer to come to the attention of the public.

Heavy metals are another type of pollutant that washes into the estuaries from the land. Although chromium, zinc, and mercury are also dangerous, lead and copper are highly poisonous and their presence in water is not readily apparent. They are present in all ocean waters and in river water that enters estuaries. They come from natural sources, such as weathering of rocks, and from human activities. Extra copper gets into water by solution from copper piping, almost universally used in plumbing, and from its use as a fungicide and algicide in swimming pools. Copper sulfate is the substance that gives pool water its beautiful blue color.

Copper also gets into water when washed off plants that have been sprayed for agricultural pests and diseases. The amount that gets into estuarine water is usually well below that considered poisonous, but it does accumulate in surface and estuarine waters in summer when the waters are warm and do not mix readily with the deeper coastal waters. At such times, copper may reach a concentration about twice that of the deeper waters. In winter, when the waters are mixed, the concentration difference disappears.

Lead, above the amount contributed by nature, comes almost entirely from tetraethyl lead added to gasoline to prevent engine knock. An additional small amount comes from the use of lead paints and agricultural sprays.

A large portion of the lead carried into rivers is bound to organic matter in the water. In this state, the lead is more soluble and available for uptake by organisms. About ten times as much lead enters the oceans from human sources as from natural weathering. Inshore waters are becoming strongly contaminated and have been found to contain about ten times as much lead as the deep waters of the central oceans, which may already contain about twice as much lead as they did in pre-industrial days. But the lead level, even in contaminated estuarine waters, is so low that a man would have to drink ten to twenty gallons a day for several months to get enough to be poisoned.

The animals that live in the water, however, are continuously exposed to the accumulating metal. Lead concentrations of five hundred to one thousand times that in the water are found in marine organisms and the concentration is increased at each step in the food chain. It is possible that animals that have adapted over the long history of the earth to the pre-industrial lead levels may be adversely affected by the present levels.

Potentially, there is a worse heavy metal situation in the salt marshes. The soils contain hydrogen sulfide from the activities of sulfur-reducing bacteria. The sulfides of copper and lead that form when water percolates down through the marsh muds at low tide are highly insoluble. Heavy metals are trapped in the mud and accumulate there. The salt marsh collects heavy metals by sulfide formation, by concentration in organisms, and by formation of complexes with organic matter. Since the marshes lie at the junction of freshwater runoff and the sea, they are further in a position to catch heavy metals before they have a chance to be diluted.

We don't know of any research on the concentrations of heavy metals in marshes. Study of the concentration of lead in waters is only beginning. There may be no reason to be concerned, but the circumstances are such that there could be a problem, or even a disaster. It would come upon us almost without warning when critical levels were reached. All pollutants are potentially dangerous.

The number and amount of pollutants already discussed are staggering, but there are still other highly dangerous pollutants, pesticides. Some of them come from the land in runoff into estuaries. Some are sprayed directly onto the marshes. Some are very stable compounds that are only very slowly broken down by biochemical activity. The pesticides are effective in extremely minute amounts and are not obviously apparent except by their deadly effects.

In the last few years, an almost incredible amount of invective has been printed about the effects of pesticides. At one extreme are those who believe that any use of pesticides is dangerous and unjustified. They ignore the importance of these chemicals in controlling plant and animal disease, in increased plant yields, and in subsequent greatly reduced consumer costs.

At the other extreme are apologists for the pesticide industry, including some government workers, who suggest that harm rarely results from the use of pesticides. A recently published statement by Louis A. McLean of the Vesicole Chemical Corporation places critics of pesticide use in two groups: those who use the controversy to sell natural foods or books they have written; and those who are compulsive, sexually maladjusted, and given to beliefs in various sorts of quackery. The latter can be distinguished by their use of the word "biocides." Since one especially significant fact about the more dangerous insecticides is that they will kill many forms of animal life, they can logically be called "biocides." The authors of this book apparently belong to both groups of critics.

Pesticides are useful and necessary in modern society. They are also dangerous. Most labels carry the skull and crossbones and warnings. All of them are of course poisonous to some extent; that is their function. The very dangerous and extremely poisonous pesticides are not distributed to the general public and rarely contaminate the environment. Another group is very dangerous, not because they are unusually poisonous as pesticides go, but because they are effective against a broad spectrum of organisms and are long lasting. DDT, endrin and dieldrin are in this group. They have a broad distribution and have caused widespread deaths among wildlife.

The discovery of DDT as an insecticide was hailed as a milestone to public health, along with the wonder drugs. DDT saved the lives of many people when it was first used during the Second World War. It prevented the spread of diseases by killing lice and mosquitoes. Its discovery stimulated pesticide research, which led to the discovery of the wide variety of substances now available.

But, it was not until sometime after DDT came into wide use that indications of harmful results began showing up. When it was used to control pests of apples, it promoted attacks of scale insects and mites which had not previously been a problem. The Nova Scotia Department of Agriculture decided that more harm than good resulted from spraying with DDT rather than other insecticides. It was also soon discovered that high concentrations of DDT would kill desirable animals, especially crustaceans such as crabs and shrimp. It has only recently been discovered, twenty years after its initial use, that DDT can be enormously concentrated as it passes along the food chain, until dosages that are extremely minute in the water or soil become concentrated enough to kill predatory birds.

DDT has become so inexpensive and useful that it has been applied all over the world. There are no areas of the earth that are not contaminated. Even penguins from Antarctica and deep sea fish have been found to contain detectable amounts of DDT.

The cahow, a bird that nests only on a few small islets at Bermuda, feeds only at sea. It is almost extinct and was even thought to be so for many years. It has clung to existence against great odds for three hundred years. Now it is apparently on its way to final extinction, doomed by DDT spread even to the open ocean by human carelessness. The near extinction of bald eagles, peregrine falcons and cooper's hawks in the eastern part of the United States within the last decade has also been credibly blamed on pesticides, especially DDT and dieldrin.

In a study of the biological concentration of DDT on a salt marsh estuarine system on Long Island, it was

found that there was little DDT in the water. Only one
part insecticide in one billion parts of water, one ppb
(part per billion), was recorded. A very different result was found for DDT in the soil, since it is nearly
insoluble in water. The marshes around the Long Island
estuary have been sprayed with DDT for twenty years.
The soil beneath S. patens marshes contained an average of thirteen pounds of DDT per acre and mud in the
ditches contained nearly three pounds per acre.

DDT in the soil serves as a reservoir from which the
water can continually extract the poison. Water carries
very little of the pesticide at any one time, but because
water is so mobile, it is continually transferring DDT
from the soil to anything that will take it out of solution.

The DDT carried by the water is extracted from it
by animals and then trapped in their fatty tissues. The
amount of concentration can be astonishing. Oysters
living in water containing one tenth part per billion
DDT will, in one month, concentrate it by seventy thousand times and have a concentration of seven parts per
million in their tissues. This is the highest amount of
DDT that raw beef fat is permitted to contain and still
be sold.

This sort of concentration occurs throughout the food
chain, although the amounts at each step are usually
less than those between the oyster and the water. An
animal must eat about ten pounds of food to increase
one pound in weight. We should expect to find about a
tenfold concentration of DDT at each step in the food
chain. But this tenfold concentration is only approxi-
mate because of the complication of the interlocking
steps in the chain.

The concentration of DDT occurs not only along the
food chain, but it occurs through time as well. A man
can kill himself with aspirin if he takes a large enough
dose. But he cannot kill himself by taking one twentieth
of a lethal dose each day for twenty days. This is
because aspirin is excreted, not stored in the body. The

Osprey nest above marsh

lethal dose of DDT approximates the lethal dose of aspirin. But, while DDT is in part changed to relatively nonpoisonous compounds and in part excreted, a considerable portion is stored in the body. A man or animal can be easily poisoned by taking nonlethal doses of DDT over a period of time.

In the study of the Long Island estuary, there was no analysis of concentrations of DDT in algae or detritus, but there was for *Spartina patens*, which showed the roots to contain nearly three ppm (parts per million) DDT while the shoots contained one third ppm.

Apparently the planktonic algae in the estuary contained appreciably less than the grass, for the zooplankton which fed on it contained only four hundredths ppm. This is as near the base of the food web as we can get with the data from this study. Of the animals that ate the zooplankton, several types of minnows were analyzed and found to contain about one ppm DDT, a concentration of twenty-five times over their food supply. In the higher levels of the food web in fish and birds, a little more than one ppm to over seventy-five ppm were found. The highest value was found in a young ring-billed gull.

Fish-eating birds, such as herons and terns, were found to have about four ppm, a fourfold concentration of DDT over their food. Birds such as gulls are scavengers and exist on a higher level in the food chain. Birds that eat birds are on a higher level yet and probably contain five to ten times more DDT concentration. The amounts in the most contaminated birds in the study were at the lethal level.

Mammals are not as sensitive to DDT poisoning as are lower animals, but they can be poisoned. It is fortunate we are mammals for we have DDT in our body fat. If the pollution of the environment with DDT continues, it is only a matter of time before mammals, too, reach the lethal concentrations. There has already been a case in which a man had considerable DDT stored in his body fat but in not a high enough concentration to cause poisoning. The man dieted, reduced his fat content and released the DDT stored there. The extra DDT in the blood put the unfortunate individual in the hospital.

The amounts of pesticide in the Long Island salt marshes are very small in absolute amounts. What is astounding is the large effect these small amounts can have. Blue crabs and fiddler crabs have become rare on the marshes since the program of DDT spraying was started. Populations of shrimp, amphipods, summer flounder, woodcock, spring peeper, osprey, and bald eagle have declined. It is a moot point whether they were directly poisoned by DDT or declined because their food was poisoned.

Since DDT accumulates in the fat of animals, it is usually present in the fat-rich eggs and sperm in higher quantities than in the adult animal. The effect of the poisons is directed to the susceptible, young stages. The decline of large birds, such as eagles and ospreys, is closely associated with the concentration of DDT in the eggs.

One recently discovered cause of nesting failure is that DDT interferes with steroid metabolism in birds, which in turn affects calcium metabolism. The birds lay eggs with thinner shells than is usual. Thin-shelled eggs are easily broken by movements of the adults, whereupon the parent no longer recognizes the egg as something to brood, but sees it instead as something to eat. We know very little about possible similar hormone interference on other animals, including man.

DDT in concentrations too small to kill animals may still affect their growth. A concentration of DDT in water of only ten parts per billion is enough to produce a sixty percent reduction in growth of young oysters. It has recently been discovered that small concentrations of DDT can also have a large inhibitory effect on algal growth, thus reducing the base of the food web on which all other organisms depend. This could very well turn out to be the most important effect of the persistent pesticides.

DDT acts on the nervous system of animals, causing them to act nervous and edgy. Birds may jump off their eggs at slight disturbances which would not excite a normal bird, or they may desert the nests entirely with little provocation. Fish may become hypersensitive to their surroundings. While they would normally swim close to a creek bank, staying under protective overhangs, they swim farther out in the open when under the influence of pesticides. As they are more visible, they are more likely to be taken by heron or other fish-eating birds. By the same token, the heron is likely to get a fish with a higher than average load of body poison.

Since amounts of DDT in the parts per billion range can be harmful to life in the marshes, it is important to relate this to the amounts used as insecticide sprays. A modest spray level would be two tenths of a pound of DDT per acre of marsh. If this is an average marsh along the central Atlantic coast and includes intertidal and high marsh areas, a normal tide would flood it to an average depth of three feet. This modest spray level would be enough to saturate the water with DDT for the following two weeks, assuming that the water is completely exchanged on each tide. Actually, much of the water that floods the marsh on one tide refloods it on the next, so that the water would be saturated for considerably more than two weeks. If the DDT did not saturate the water, which is more likely, the amount would be spread over a much larger volume for a much longer time, at least six months. Most marshes that are sprayed are sprayed more than once a year, making DDT always present in seriously large amounts.

Fortunately, the average salt marsh is less contaminated than the Long Island marsh mentioned earlier. On the average, oysters from the East Coast contain about one tenth ppm DDT with more in the summer and less in winter. This variation reflects variation in DDT use on the land. In estuaries that receive drainage from urban centers, the DDT level remains high throughout the year. This no doubt reflects the sort of pollution to which people living in the urban centers are subjected.

What has been said about DDT can also be said of many other pesticides. Some are even more dangerous and have not done more harm because they are expensive or less widely used for other reasons. There is a potential in these chemicals to do damage to the salt marshes that can never be undone. Rather than look at the amounts contaminating the soil and water, we should look at the levels of concentration at several levels of the food chain. Oysters which are continually pumping water through their bodies give a good indication of current levels of pollution. The highest animals in the food chain give an indication of how much cumulative harm has been done. Humans, living on a diet including meat and sea foods, are next in line.

There is yet another type of pollution. More and more estuarine water is being used to cool certain phases of industry. Rivers have always been preferred for this purpose but rivers are used to a large extent already and there is little room for new industry. Industry is now turning to the edge of the sea, especially the power industry. Very large plants are being built using seawater as a coolant. Vast quantities of water will be heated a few degrees in the cooling process. Animals and plants living in the water will naturally be affected. It is very difficult to predict what might happen in this situation. We believe that life in the heated water will proceed a little faster and resemble a similar estuary perhaps a hundred miles to the south But the northern estuary, even though heated, will still be surrounded by cold waters and animals adapted to cold waters.

Perhaps changes will be to the good. There is a natural example in Northumberland Strait between Prince Edward Island and Nova Scotia of an area appreciably warmer than its surroundings. There is warm water for swimming and the only oysters growing north of Cape Cod exist there. A warmed estuary somewhere in northern New England might achieve the same beneficial results and produce a commercial crop of oysters in water that was previously too cold to support it. There is a difference however. The artificially warmed water would be warmer throughout the year, unlike Northumberland Strait, which freezes over in the winter. It is possible that the warming might favor a clam predator that was previously checked by cold winters.

A danger of thermal pollution has appeared in connection with some of the new power stations along the New England coast. Fish are generally attracted to warm water. They will seek water that is only slightly cooler than that which will kill them. We do not know why. Temperature changes in the water at the outlets from power plants can be very large and sudden with the outpouring of heated water so that schools of fish swimming nearby can quickly be engulfed by lethal waters.

The Massachusetts Department of Marine Fisheries has already found large kills of young menhaden at the outlet of a new generating plant. These fish were killed by chlorine which had been added to the cooling system to prevent fouling. But they were initially attracted to the fatal region by the warmed water. We still know very little about the effects of thermal pollution and must proceed with great caution.

Of all types of pollution, the most alarming in terms of extent and danger, both to the marshes and to men, is undoubtedly that resulting from the use of persistent pesticides.

14. Mosquito Control

SALT MARSHES ARE NOTORIOUS FOR THEIR PRODUCTION of biting flies: midges, greenheads, and mosquitoes. Probably the single most troublesome insect, certainly the most troublesome marsh mosquito, is *Aedes sollicitans*. This mosquito does not lay eggs on the water surface as do many others. It lays eggs where they will remain dry for at least a day before they are flooded.

Conditions suitable for *Aedes sollicitans* occur near land on the high marsh where the mud is dry part of the time but where small depressions are filled with water by spring tides or by rain. Eggs laid on the mud when these depressions are dry develop and then hatch upon flooding. Once the mosquitoes emerge as adults, they will fly considerable distances from the marsh in search of prey. Anyone who lives near a marsh that produces numbers of mosquitoes demands that something be done to control them.

Insect control methods fall into two groups: those that attack the insect pests directly without immediately changing the marsh, such as spraying; and those that change the marsh so that it is no longer suitable as a habitat for the pest, such as ditching.

There are serious objections to almost all of the control techniques as they have been used in the past. We have already dealt with the disadvantages of spraying with persistent pesticides. Ditching, as it has been most widely used, in the high marshes of the northeast, is damaging in that it drains the entire marsh. Pools are emptied that formerly attracted wildlife. General drainage can also change the composition of the marsh, accelerating the changes toward high marsh, even to the point of allowing the invasion of shrubby *Iva*, an important plant in the border between land and marsh.

The opposite of draining, that is, building dikes to create impoundments near the land, is also used. Water is pumped into the diked areas from estuaries. Since the water level in these pools does not fluctuate, *A. sollicitans* cannot find a spot on which to lay its eggs. Eggs that are laid on the pool edges and eggs laid by other species are quickly destroyed by minnows that colonize the impoundments. Although this technique makes the marsh unsuitable for mosquitoes, it also makes it unsuitable for *Spartina*. Eventually the marsh is destroyed. The impounded water is cut off from the estuary which no longer derives nutrients from the area.

Fire has also been used as an insect control in burning high marsh areas in late summer and early fall. This is directed against greenhead flies rather than mosquitoes and does destroy many of their eggs. But it kills other animals as well. Much of the marsh grass production that would otherwise go to feed estuarine animals burns.

Fortunately, modifications of these control techniques have been worked out that give good results with a minimum of damage to the marsh and associated estuaries. They require the willingness to spend money and men who understand enough marsh ecology to do the job correctly. The best example of good mosquito control that we know of is found in the Cape Cod Mosquito Control Project under the direction of Mr. Doane. The Project concentrates on keeping marsh pools and ponds accessible to marsh minnows that feed on mosquito larvae. The workers cut shallow ditches from the ponds which are deepened out toward creeks. Because the ditches are shallow next to the ponds, the ponds retain water at low tide. Fish can swim into them through the ditches at high tide and remain in them at low tide. The ditches remain open for from five to ten years, after which time they must be dug out again. The ponds may also gradually fill in with sediment carried by water flooding through the ditches. When this happens, they must also be dug out. If they are allowed to remain full of silt, the fish die during periods of low tide and mosquitoes again lay eggs on the periodically flooded surface of the mud.

Adult insects can be treated with fogs of nonpersistent insecticides. A fog, which can be effective only when used during windless periods, can kill adult insects and still leave very little residue on the marsh surface. The amount that does settle is so finely divided that it is rapidly destroyed by sunlight and air before it has a chance to cause damage. Amounts of insecticide too small to kill insects can be effective in driving them away from the sprayed area. This technique is especially useful against greenheads that stay on the marsh. Fogging can drive the flies to other areas of the marsh where they are less obnoxious. An added advantage to the technique is that since it does not kill insects, there is no buildup of resistance to the spray. Fogging on the Cape is not used on any sort of regular schedule but only in response to specific insect annoyance.

While the insecticides with a long life are harmful to the marsh, there are others available which are short-lived. Some of the new organophosphate insecticides are effective against insect pests and relatively nontoxic to fish, birds, and mammals at concentrations needed for insect control. Most important from the conservationist's point of view, the compounds are destroyed rather quickly. If they can be applied in such a way as to kill the insects before their effectiveness disappears, they will be very useful. They are being studied especially for their effectiveness against larvae.

This combination of control techniques is almost

ideal, DDT has not been used on Cape Cod salt
marshes for years and still mosquitoes are not a problem. The ponds are not drained and remain to attract
waterfowl and shorebirds. Unfortunately, even though
the Cape Cod method is very effective, it is not widely
used. Such techniques are possibly too expensive to use
on a large scale as would be required to deal with all
the salt marshes in New Jersey, but they should certainly be used on special small marshes, surrounded by
inhabited uplands, where mosquito control is necessary
but the marsh is to be preserved in as undisturbed a
state as possible. This prescription fits all of the
marshes north of southern New Jersey as well as some
in the southeast.

Along most of the southeast coast, a different combination of techniques is necessary to provide insect control at reasonable cost. The impoundment technique is
useful if limited to those areas of the marsh near land.
This is the part of the marsh most likely to contain the
temporary pools necessary for mosquito breeding as
well as the part closest to human habitation. It is also
the part of the marsh where the grass production is
probably least available to the estuary and therefore
least missed when destroyed. Impoundments have the
advantage that they are very attractive to waterfowl.
There are indications that the cost of impoundment
may be more than returned by the money spent by
hunters attracted by the ducks and geese lured to the
impoundments. In this case, the mosquito control is
free.

Another possibility is the use of these impoundments
for aquiculture. If shrimp or even "trash fish" could be
raised in large amounts in the mosquito impoundments,
they could not only pay for themselves but return a
profit.

Ditching to drain the marsh probably does more
harm than good except in *Juncus roemerianus*, Southern black rush, marshes. These marshes are only irregu-

larly flooded by tides. Their productivity has not been carefully studied but it is probably not readily available to estuarine animals. Ditching opens the marsh to flooding by the tides. This encourages growth of *Spartina* along the ditches, makes the productivity more readily available to aquatic organisms, and provides open water space which is used by waterfowl. These benefits are all in addition to the main advantage, the prevention of temporary pools in which mosquitoes can breed.

With these two control methods, using impoundments and ditching, much of the mosquito problem could be solved in those places where the preferred Cape Cod method is too expensive. There would still be areas where too many mosquitoes for comfort would exist, and where other marsh insects made pests of themselves. In those areas, the best solution would be to attack the insect pests at the point of the problem rather than where they breed. Nonpersistent chemicals can be applied as fogs to kill and drive away noxious insects.

Electric insect traps will keep local areas free of all sorts of night-flying insects. Persistent pesticides can even be used if carefully applied to building interiors but with the warning that they only be applied to surfaces, such as ceilings, where they will not be touched by the inhabitants. Aside from this special application, which is principally for prevention of disease carried by insects, the persistent pesticides should not be used at all.

Insects will still be a problem out on the marshes. Fishermen and nature lovers will risk being bitten. The only rational solution to their problem at the pesent time is the use of repellents, spread or sprayed directly on the body. These work very well. It is only by the use of repellents that much of the scientific work on marshes, on which this book is based, is accomplished.

There are other insect control techniques which are not used on salt marshes but some of which may, in the future, provide the best method for insect control, especially on the extensive southeast marshes. One that has been tried is the use of natural parasites. Another with a promising future is the use of "third generation" insecticides.

The use of parasites to control insects is not a new idea. A parasitic wasp which preys on greenhead flies was introduced in Texas several decades ago. Under good conditions the parasite caused a fifty percent reduction of the flies. This percentage was not considered high enough and the attempt was abandoned. Insects can also be controlled by disease organisms, an example being the milky disease of Japanese beetles. Again, the advantage of these techniques is that they are specific against only the insects that the disease or parasite attacks, and are harmless to other organisms. But they are often expensive and there may be no known disease or parasite that will do the job.

Another technique involves tricking the insect pest. Screwworms, which attack cattle, have been controlled by raising large numbers of males and then sterilizing them by radiation. The sterilized males are released into their environment. Females have less chance of meeting a normal, fertile male and so there is a decrease in offspring the following year. If the number of sterile males is kept high, the population rapidly declines to extinction. Another trick depends on attracting one sex to a trap baited with specific sounds and smells of the other.

A new development in pest control hopes to make use of third generation pesticides. First generation pesticides are typified by arsenic and nicotine poisons and second generation pesticides by DDT. Third generation insecticides rely on insect hormones to reduce the population.

Juvenile hormones are necessary for the normal development of insects. Insects grow in size during their immature stages, then cease growth, transform into adults, and become sexually mature. Juvenile hormone prevents transformation to the adult condition when the insect is still young. When the proper larval development is completed, juvenile hormone production stops and the insect matures. Juvenile hormone, applied externally when internal production is stopping, also prevents maturation. Since the treated insect doesn't mature, it cannot reproduce and so is eliminated. Because the chemicals are specific insect hormones, they have no effect on other forms of life. Because they are essential to a part of the life cycle, the insect cannot develop an immunity to them.

Third generation insecticides seem the ideal solution to the pest problem, especially in the light of the danger of first and second generation insecticides. Unfortunately, they are just being developed and are not yet available. Difficulties remain in the development. The known natural hormones are impossible to manufacture at this time and affect too wide a range of insects. Some of the substitutes so far synthesized also have too wide an effect. Most insects in nature are harmless if not beneficial. Indiscriminate destruction of insects would be a calamity.

A possible way out of this dilemma has been suggested by the recent discovery of a synthetic insect hormone occurring in paper made of balsam fir, the principal source of pulpwood in the northern United States and Canada. It was found that this hormone inhibited the maturation in one family of bugs. The bugs had been successfully raised in Europe in containers lined with paper. When they were brought to the United States, attempts made to raise the bugs in a like manner failed consistently. Many experiments later it was discovered that the bugs reacted to the synthetic insect hormone in balsam fir paper which was absent in European papers. Presumably, at one time, a bug of this family attacked the balsam which countered with this defense. This is a guess as that particular bug is now extinct or no longer attacks the balsam fir for obvious reasons. If balsam fir can produce an imitation hormone that acts on only one family of insects, it should be possible to produce other imitation hormones.

If it becomes possible to spray large areas at reasonable cost and prevent not all the mosquitoes but only the mosquitoes on a particular area from maturing, then mosquitoes will no longer be a problem on salt marshes, or anywhere else.

15. Human Destruction of Marshes

NO ONE KNOWS HOW MUCH SALT MARSH EXISTED along the Atlantic coast of North America before the Europeans arrived. No matter how much was here, the settlers began to change the existing amount almost immediately. The marsh was increased when erosion made new shallows which were soon invaded by marsh grass. The marsh was decreased when it suffocated under loads of eroded silt brought in by river floods. The marsh was decreased when it was dug out to widen navigation channels and it was decreased when it was filled to make waterfront property.

Old Boston set an example of marsh filling which was followed by many other cities as they grew up along the East Coast. The original area of the Boston peninsula, which protruded into the harbor like a thin-handled club, was about four hundred and seventy acres. There were about seventy acres of salt marsh closely associated with the head of the club. Between Boston and its neighboring city, Cambridge, ran the Charles River. Surrounding it was a wide area of shallow water and marsh. At least four hundred acres of salt marsh existed in this area, called Back Bay.

Small towns were established around Boston which still exist today as separate cities but which are included in the general Boston Area. There are at present about 3240 acres of city real estate in an area that contains old Boston, Roxbury and Back Bay. The area considered is roughly bounded to the southeast by Albany

Street in Boston; on the south by a line from the end of Albany Street over to and along Longwood Avenue in Roxbury, the next village landward; on the west by a line from the crossing of Longwood Avenue and Muddy River to Boston University Bridge; and on the north by a line from the Charles River around the north end of Boston into South Bay and back to Albany Street again. When the Puritans arrived to settle this area, there existed only 1185 acres of dry land on which to build. Four hundred eighty-five acres of the present 3240 acres were salt marsh and 1570 acres were shallow water which was part marsh, part mud and sand flat, and part open water even at low tide. There was a gain of 2055 acres of dry land made by filling the marshes and lowlands. This filling increased the area of solid land about 2.7 times.

Being a natural seaport, Boston was destined to be crowded with men almost immediately. In a more natural, less populated situation, the salt marshes surrounding the town would have grown instead of decreased. Newly cleared farms would have contributed dirt and sand to the streams, which would carry it to the sea to be deposited on the low-lying land or shallow harbor bottom.

Where there is a large population and little land, the land automatically becomes very valuable. Since the available ground was used up early in the settlement, there was great stress to make more.

In 1641, the first marshes were dug and filled to make the Town Cove. Dock Square, now a third of a mile from the nearest water, was then at the head of the cove. The following year a more extensive marsh in Shelter Cove was partly dug out, and partly filled in, to make wharf space. The marsh, some of which belonged to the first Governor of Massachusetts, John Winthrop, stretched from Post Office Square to the Shawmut Bank.

A yet larger marsh of some fifty acres lay on the north side of town. This was diked off a few years later

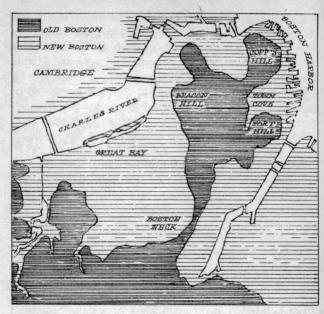

Map of Boston

and used as a millpond in the operation of tidal mills for grinding corn and sawing lumber.

Boston was founded in 1630. It took only fifteen years before every marsh enclosed in the town boundaries had been tampered with in some way.

Further filling of the marsh waited for some time. The town grew toward the west. Pressure for new land grew too, but it was not relieved for over a hundred years. In 1794, marshes that lay where the Public Gardens are now were granted by the town for the construction of ropewalks. A few years later, the widening of Boston neck was begun by filling in marsh and flats that lay to the south of Washington Street.

About the same time, the millpond that had been made from marsh was filled in with gravel taken from the top of Beacon Hill, one of the three low mountains on which Boston was built. Boston accomplished in a short time by direct effort what colonists in the middle Atlantic states allowed to happen over a much longer period by using careless agricultural methods. They took land from the high spots to fill in the coastline.

Beacon Hill was cut down by sixty feet. In return, fifty acres of land were constructed near the center of the city. What is now Causeway Street in front of Boston Garden was the dam of the millpond which lay between Washington and Merrimac Streets.

With the old millpond filled, the plan was soon developed for the creation of a much larger set of ponds to provide power for new mills. The plan called for the damming of Back Bay. There was considerable opposition as the dam would cut the bay off from free circulation with the sea. The opposition was put down and the dam completed in 1821. The part of the bay next to Boston Common became the receiving basin. The full basin, which filled at high tide, was the marshy part of Back Bay.

The large number of mills that this ambitious scheme foresaw never came into being in Boston. Instead, they were built on Merrimack River in Lowell and Lawrence. But the dam was built. Quite soon the water next to the Common became stagnant and certainly less pleasant than it had been when it was open to the flushing tides.

At first the receiving basin was allowed to go dry at low tide but the dust created by drying the flats became such a nuisance that the practice was stopped. At this time, the area was still pleasant to look at, with marshes and flats visible from the toll road on the dam leading to the Common and to the capitol building on top of Beacon Hill.

Soon the basin was cut into several pieces by the building of rail lines into Boston. The flow of water was further reduced, which caused further stagnation. The fouling of the bay was heightened when a city dump was built on one side and when a large sewer line was allowed to empty into the receiving basin.

It was small wonder that by 1850, the Board of Health described the area as offensive and injurious. Since land was again at a premium around the bay, the solution decided upon to rid the city of the putrid basin was to fill it in. Filling began in 1858. Gravel and sand were brought by rail from Needham and supplemented with the ever growing deposit of trash from the city.

The portion of the receiving basin nearest the city was filled first. It was not until 1882, twenty-four years after filling started, that the receiving basin was completely obliterated.

The basin had been enclosed by two dams: the mill dam on the north, and the cross dam on the west. The mill dam ran along the present route of Beacon Street. The cross dam ran along Massachusetts Avenue from Beacon Street to about Boylston Street where it met the high ground known as Gravely Point. The present Prudential Center occupies what was the western part of the basin.

This effort still left most of the original high marsh unfilled. The marsh lay to the west of Gravely Point. To the eyes of Bostonians, it was a wasteland. And a wasteland it soon became. Circulation was restricted with the filling of such a large portion of the bay. Now that there were a large number of people living in the area, the sewage load from Roxbury, Brookline, and Brighton that the marshy area received was sufficient to transform it completely. What had once been a pleasant site on which farmers cut salt hay was by 1880 a foul cesspool. It was said that even the hardy eel could not survive there.

This high marsh was drained and filled. A little foresight was used and portions were made into park areas. Simmons College, Back Bay Fens, and everything between the Fens and Brookline Street, including Fenway

Park, home of the Boston Red Sox, sit on that old marsh. By the beginning of the twentieth century, all traces of the old marshes and mud flats were gone, although a brook still courses through the Fens, marking the trace of the old tidal river through the marshes.

Marshes are generally considered useless land that must be made useful as quickly as possible. "Useful," of course, means destruction of the marsh in most cases and conversion of the area to ground on which people can stand, and water on which they can float boats. Present estimates are that salt marshes are being destroyed at a rate of more than one percent per year. Figures are very difficult to obtain for original tracts of salt marsh and are based on deduction ·from old records. From about the turn of this century, records have been kept by various agencies concerned with fisheries, water birds, and navigation.

The first reasonably complete survey of the area of tidal wetland in the United States was made in 1922 by the Department of Agriculture. Listed were 7,363,000 acres of tidal marsh. This figure was recorded in the *Yearbook of Agriculture* for 1923, and unfortunately, it is impossible to discover exactly what type of land was then included under the heading "tidal marsh." Probably more land was considered tidal marsh than we consider marshes in the context of this book.

In 1954, a survey was made by the Fish and Wildlife Service of coastal salt flats and shallow sounds and bays, including everything above low tide water. Five million two hundred ninety thousand acres were counted as coastal saline areas. Since this figure encompasses mud flats and other areas without plant cover, it undoubtedly covers more land than that included in the 1922 survey. On the basis of these figures, at the very minimum, the country has lost over two million acres of productive shallow coastal water and marsh, more than one quarter of the total, in the course of only thirty-two years. Another set of figures for only the Atlantic coast made by the Fish and Wildlife Service puts the loss for this region at over one half million acres during the first half of this century.

In 1964, the marshes in the northeast were resurveyed and changes in the ten years recorded. The loss of marshes varied enormously from state to state. Loss was quite closely correlated with the development of great population centers along the East Coast, the northeast megapolis. The marshes in the less heavily populated states were in better condition and less damaged than those in densely populated areas.

The great urban development, stretching from north of Boston, south to Washington, D.C., and beyond, has not yet made itself felt strongly in Maine. In the years between 1955 and 1964, only one percent of Maine's 15,500 acres of marshlands was damaged by human activities. In the same ten years, New Hampshire lost slightly more than one percent of her 6,000 acres. However, the pressure in New Hampshire has already become very great and is increasing as megapolis extends into the New Hampshire coastal area. The desirable uplands along this shore have already been largely developed, resulting in a decrease in waterfowl as the birds avoid, to some extent, marshes around which there are large numbers of people.

The development of the uplands, with its inevitable increased erosion, has also reduced the value of the marshes to fisheries by converting areas of highly productive *Spartina alterniflora* to the less productive *S. patens*. The greatest danger is developing now as pressure for filling the marshes to support housing is reaching ever higher levels.

In the seventeenth century, these marshes were so valuable that armed men from Massachusetts came to take hay from the New Hampshire marshes, about which the New Hampshire citizens complained bitterly. In the twentieth century, the heirs of those early marsh defenders are unable to agree on whether or not they will preserve those marshes. The town of Hampton has a plan to fill and develop three hundred acres or about five percent of the existing marshes in the state. There is a growing number of citizens who oppose the plan and wish to preserve the marshes as marshes.

The Massachusetts coastline is well within the heavily populated megapolis region. Massachusetts has lost about twenty percent of her tidal marshes during the course of her history and about two and one half percent of this occurred in the ten years between the two surveys. Most of the losses were due to housing developments, but the use of marshlands for dumps, making roads, parking places, and approaches for bridges accounted for a significant part of the total. About forty-two thousand acres remain.

Rhode Island has only a small area of salt marshes, less than two thousand acres. Between 1955 and 1964, it lost more than five percent of its marshes, to a large extent by construction of roads, bridges, and parking lots. Intensive construction has destroyed or doomed all of the marshes in the upper Narragansett Bay. The small number of the remaining marshes are made all the more valuable because of their scarcity.

In Connecticut, the loss of marshlands has been even higher than in Rhode Island. In the ten years between the two surveys, over twelve percent of the marshes were destroyed. Since 1914, when the first inventory of coastal wetlands in Connecticut was conducted, nearly forty percent of the total marsh area had been destroyed. Less than fifteen thousand acres remained in the state.

The closer the marsh lay to New York City, the more likely it was that it was destroyed by the spreading urban complex. Most of the marshes were lost by filling for houses, industrial sites, airports, and dumps, among other reasons. A significant portion has been destroyed by being mined as a source of sand and gravel for road building and for use as an aggregate in concrete. The largest part of the cost of supplying sand and gravel is the cost in getting it from the source to the consumer.

Dealers try to substitute cheap water transportation for trucking whenever possible. A source of material where it can be loaded directly into barges is ideal from their viewpoint. As a result there has been great pressure for dredging marshes for sand and gravel. This has often been accomplished under the pretext of improving navigation and making marinas. In one case in Connecticut, a firm tried to obtain a permit to dig a trench three hundred feet wide and thirty feet deep, one and a half miles long, to be used as an access channel for small boats to a marina site. This channel, which would have been big enough to float passenger liners, was obviously designed more as a source of sand and gravel than a channel for small boats.

If the losses of marshes in Connecticut are impressive and increase as they go toward the central city region of megapolis New York, the losses in Long Island are even more shocking. Nearly thirty percent of the Long Island marshes disappeared in the ten years between the two surveys. Nearly all of the marshes in Bronx County disappeared, along with fifty percent in Kings County, thirty percent in Queens County, thirty percent in Nassau County, and seventeen percent in Suffolk County. Although the percentages lost in Nassau and Suffolk Counties are less than the counties closer to the city, the total amounts of marshes destroyed in these outer reaches of Long Island are greater. The percentages are smaller because of the much greater area of marsh remaining toward the eastern end of Long Island.

The rate of destruction has not slowed since the end of 1964 when the report was made. Filling and dredging of the remaining thirty thousand acres has continued at an alarming rate.

New Jersey has far more salt marsh than any of the states so far considered. Two hundred ninety-six thousand acres existed along the shoreline in 1895. Of this, two hundred thirty-two thousand acres, or less than eighty percent, were left in 1964. As well as the actual

Aerial view of a marsh

destruction of marsh, much remaining marsh, particularly around the region of New York City, has deteriorated because of siltation and pollution. This is particularly apparent in the Hackensack Meadows region and the shores of Raritan River. There are also ten thousand acres of southern New Jersey marshes which have been diked for the production of salt hay. The dike prevents free access of tidal waters to this area and its contribution to estuarine production is therefore greatly reduced.

Delaware is the most southern of the states surveyed in 1954 by the Fish and Wildlife Service which was resurveyed in 1964 and for which we can state the loss of salt marsh during the interval. Delaware, which lost little before that time, lost nearly four percent of its marshes in the ten year period. The loss was due mainly to marshes being used as spoils areas for dredging in the Wilmington region. In 1964 Delaware was left with about 115,000 acres of salt marshes.

Much of the development in Delaware, as in other states of the northeast, occurs in small amounts so that the destruction of marshes is not noticed except by those who are immediately concerned. But the small destructions accumulate until large significant amounts of marsh have disappeared. In the period between 1954 and 1965, forty-five thousand acres of salt marsh were destroyed between Maine and Delaware. About one third of this amount was suffocated by dredging spoils and navigation channel maintenance. One quarter of the amount was filled for construction of buildings. The building of roads, bridges, marinas, industries, airports, and town dumps accounts for most of the remainder. The argument that an increased tax base is required is used again and again to justify the destruction of marshes for housing developments. But invariably, increased housing increases rather than decreases the tax burden on everyone. Taxes in larger cities or towns are always larger than those in otherwise comparable but smaller units. A valid argument based upon economy for everyone, not just a favored few, would favor marsh preservation.

The problem of deposition of dredging spoils is going to get progressively worse. In Delaware Bay, as everywhere, the spoils were formerly dumped overboard. Much of the dumped material quickly washed back into the channel from which it had been removed, making the maintenance of the channel a continuous struggle. Steady dredging removed sixteen to eighteen million cubic yards of material each year to maintain a thirty-eight foot deep channel up to Philadelphia.

Now the spoil is pumped into diked areas where the mud and sand settle out, leaving the water to wash back into the bay. Only eight to ten million yards are now dredged per year and the channel is kept about forty-two feet deep. Since it costs about one dollar a yard for dredging, there is an eight million dollar saving and a four to five foot deeper channel is maintained. This sounds fine until you realize that almost all of the spoil disposal areas used to be salt marshes. The productivity of these marshes is now lost. What will happen when these spoil areas are full? Will the agencies preserving marshes for their biological value be able to resist the pressure to destroy those marshes in turn? And what will happen when even deeper channels are desired?

Tankers are now being built which will draw seventy feet of water. There isn't that much water in the channels into any major East Coast port and these tankers are designed to be loaded and emptied from offshore moorings connected by pipelines to shore. Presumably larger ships for other cargoes will follow if the experience with tankers is successful.

Chambers of commerce will press for deeper channels into their ports. If this seems like a far distant worry, think how many people one hundred years ago would have ever imagined dredging a deepwater channel all the way from Houston, Texas, to make a major port of what used to be a small city at the head of winding Buffalo Bayou. A distance of fifty miles of shallow water lay between it and the Gulf of Mexico. There is little doubt that cities will continue to try to improve their port facilities, partly by dredging deeper navigation channels. Marshes will continue to be subjected to pressures to use them as spoil areas.

Virginia and North Carolina each have one hundred and fifty thousand to two hundred thousand acres of salt marsh. The marshes along this area of the coast begin to be less important to waterfowl than those to the north as the birds tend to go inland to the freshwater lakes and marshes. However, these southern salt marshes are very important to the fish they support.

South Carolina has over half a million acres of salt marsh and Georgia nearly four hundred thousand acres. Florida leads every other state along the Atlantic with over half a million acres each of mangrove swamp and of grassy salt marsh.

There is less readily available information about the destruction of salt marshes for the states from Maryland south to Florida. We know that Maryland has lost between five and ten percent of its more than two hundred thousand acres of salt marsh within the last fifteen years. It is within the region of great population pressure. Most of the loss has occurred on both sides of the upper Chesapeake Bay where development for homes and industry is rapid. Fortunately, there are still large areas of salt marsh remaining to the south, along the eastern shore of Chesapeake Bay, which are important to fish and wintering waterfowl.

There are still vast areas of salt marsh along the southeast coast. Nevertheless, considerable damage has been done to these abundant marshes. It is estimated that from twenty-five to thirty percent have either been destroyed or altered enough to reduce their value for fishes and wildlife. A recent survey for North Carolina shows that four and one half percent of the marshes have been filled and destroyed and twenty-three and one half percent altered. In a few cases, the alteration has been for the better, such as ditching to open *Juncus* marshes to tides or the creation of artificial potholes. But usually, the alteration reduces the natural value of the marsh for fish and wildlife.

You have only to investigate the cost of building lots for summer and year-round houses along the southeast coast to realize that the demand for land there is already very great. Once these building areas on the uplands are gone, the pressure to fill and use the marsh for development will be nearly irresistible as far as any private owner is concerned. Even though this coastal area of the southeast is out of the megapolis region and is relatively lightly populated, the increased length of vacation season, the excellence of saltwater fishing, and the increased mobility of the American population pose a threat to the preservation of its salt marshes.

A great despoiler of southern marshes is dredging. The inland waterway along the South Carolina coast has used or is planning to use about ten percent of the marsh area for disposal of spoils. In Charleston Harbor, some ten thousand acres have been covered, that is, most of the marsh that existed there. Dredging is particularly extensive along the southeast coast because of the great amount of sediment carried into the coastal waters by rivers.

A future great danger to the entire coastal region in the southeast is mining. Much of the area is underlaid by phosphate rock which can be profitably mined. A plan to mine the bottom of the Pamlico River in North Carolina has been, at least temporarily, shelved due to objections from the Department of Interior. Another plan to mine an area for three miles on either side of the present beachline between Savanah and St. Catherines Sound, Georgia, has not yet been approved at the time of this writing, but the plan has the backing of Georgia's governor. This scheme includes diking the area, removing the over-burden which is mostly marsh, and strip-mining the phosphate rock. The process would destroy about one third of Georgia's salt marshes. Such a tremendous loss would be felt by commercial and sport fishermen along the entire Atlantic seaboard.

These large schemes attract a great deal of attention because they threaten so much marsh at one stroke. In many cases, opposition to the schemes can marshal enough force to prevent the damage. But perhaps a greater danger is the piecemeal filling and dredging of a bit of marsh here and a bit there. Any one piece is too small to attract a great deal of attention but the cumulative destruction can be just as great as that caused by a few large projects. Until any area has at least statewide planning for marsh conservation, the future of salt marshes can be no better than gloomy.

Flordia started out with large acreages of salt marsh in the north and mangrove swamps with associated salt marshes to the landward side of the swamps in the south. Florida can also boast as much coastal saltwater fishing as anywhere in the country. These two facts are closely related. Much of the productivity supporting the fishing activity depends on shallow water coastal areas and their associated salt marshes.

In spite of the importance of the shallow water areas to Florida, the destruction of these areas has been great. Florida's popularity as a vacation spot and retirement haven is also a curse for its salt marshes. The pressures for shoreline development have been enormous. The resulting large-scale dredging, filling, bridging, and bulkheading have resulted in great losses of productivity and fertility along the shore. Although we don't have figures for losses of productive shallow water and marsh areas directly, there are figures from the Florida State Board of Conservation showing a drastic decline in the commercial catches of several species of fish in Palm Beach County as a result of dredging and siltation of the brackish water lagoon known as Lake Worth.

A large portion of the Florida mangroves has been protected by the creation of the Everglades National Park but other large areas, especially along the eastern shore and the Keys, have been destroyed so that houses might be built on the former swamplands.

In colonial days and continuing into the early twentieth century, marshes were valuable for the hay they produced. They were ranked along with upland meadows and woodlots as important pieces of land in the colonists' way of life. They were often traded between owners. Their specific value was frequently recorded in early deeds, as being a piece of salt meadow containing a certain number, more or less, of loads. The loads were loads of salt hay. This was understood by all and left unstated.

It is now assumed by most people who bother to think of it at all that marshes are valueless at best. On the debit side of the evaluation, mismanaged marshes are considered to smell bad and to breed noxious insects. Less hostile but more dangerous opinion simply considers them land, unusable in its present condition, standing in the way of progress, the sooner filled the better. A typical statement made in about 1920 concerning the salt marshes of Cape Cod states that they were vastly important in the old days for the hay they produced. It was expected that, in the future, they would be diked and reclaimed and be like little patches of Netherlands lowlands.

It isn't logical or even likely that many polders will ever be created from New England or other salt marshes. Better and cheaper agricultural land is readily available elsewhere. Unfortunately, we are all too familiar with the spectacle of one government agency encouraging and helping farmers to drain land which destroys prairie freshwater marshes and potholes, while another agency spends money to recreate marshes and potholes for the preservation of wildlife. The East Coast salt marshes are not immune to the results of this sort of governmental schizophrenia.

Along the south Atlantic coast, marshes were diked for rice production and cattle grazing. Rice is no longer grown in these diked marshes, and when drainage was improved so that other crops could be grown in the old rice lands, many of the soils became so acid from the oxidation of sulfides that they were useless for crops. We have seen diked and drained marshes that grew nothing but a bumper crop of dust, a mere twenty years after the "improvements" were made.

The decision to stop using marshes for purposes for which they are not suitable must come from all the people. The local owners will ordinarily want to drain them, dredge them, or fill them in order to get the maximum value for their land. Local chambers of commerce, typically lacking any understanding of biological values, support the owners. But the maximum value of the marshes to the country is as salt marshes. Unless this value is realized and action to save marshes is taken soon, the remaining marshes will quickly disappear.

16. Solutions and Suggestions

THE DANGERS TO SALT MARSHES STEM FROM HUMAN activities, not natural processes. We destroy wetlands and shallow water bottoms directly by dredging, filling, and building. Indirectly we destroy them by pollution. Much of this destruction is simply foolish. The marsh would often have been much more valuable as a marsh than it is in its subsequent desecrated form.

The increase in population pressure along the coast will inevitably destroy more and more of the frail marsh estuarine system. We do not propose the preservation of the marshes simply for the sake of their preservation. Instead, we regard them in light of their benefit to the growing population. The benefit of marshes will accrue to everyone, not only those who venture onto the surface of marshes but to fishermen along the coast and to consumers of fishery products who may live far inland.

Some destruction is inevitable. Even for those marshes preserved as wildlife areas, an access must be constructed so that people who want to enjoy these pieces of nature can do so. Roads must be built to the marshes, along the edges of marshes, and to impoundments that are designed for mosquito control and waterfowl hunting. Also, building roads to boat-launching ramps so that the network of creeks and rivers in the wetlands can be enjoyed is not only a convenience but a preservative: damage to the marshes will be less if adequate access is provided from the waterside.

But after having conceded that we cannot avoid destroying some marshes, how are we to decide which should be destroyed and which preserved? And by what means shall we preserve them? It is obvious that overall planning is necessary. The very minimum of planning could be approached on the state level, but a more rational approach demands planning on the national level, as it is the whole marsh system with its high productivity, rather than individual marshes, that needs preservation. Overall planning demands that we have a classification of the value and importance of every area of marsh along the coast.

A start has been made on a classification of the coastal wetlands. On the federal level, surveys have been made and are being made by the Fish and Wildlife Service. The Clean Water Restoration Act of 1966 directed the Department of the Interior to report to Congress by November 3, 1969, on pollution in tidal waters. This survey will include studies of water quality, sedimentation, sources of pollution, control needs, quality standards, uses—including recreation and habitat for animals, as well as use in navigation, mining, dredging, and filling. This survey is under way at present. In the autumn of 1968 another bill passed Congress which asks the Department of the Interior for a second report, by January 30, 1970, on the nation's estuaries. This will contain recommendations for protecting, conserving, and restoring estuaries to maintain a balance between conservation and development. This bill guarantees power of decision to the states.

Once the marshes have been surveyed and recommendations made, decisions must be made concerning the use to which the existing marshes and estuaries should be put. Preservation is certainly the desirable thing for all of the *Spartina alterniflora* marshes, which are the most valuable with respect to the productivity of the coastline. Many *S. patens* marshes are also of high value. Other marshes would perhaps be best preserved for use in aquiculture. Still others could be considered less valuable, and it is these which will pose the problems. Should they be preserved, or even made productive, or should they be filled for construction or industrial development?

One essential to a rational decision as to which marshes should be preserved is continued scientific research into the value and best use of salt marshes. We have only begun to understand the interrelationship of the animals and plants that make the salt marshes and associated estuaries one of the most productive areas on earth.

Along with deciding which areas to preserve, we must concentrate the responsibility of decision in fewer agencies of government. At the present time, fish and game agencies are responsible for conservation of wildlife along the shores. The U.S. Corps of Engineers, state engineering departments, and public works departments are responsible for dredging, channel maintenance, and dock building. Public health agencies are responsible for pollution control, and so on. If the responsibility were primarily in one agency, the problem of making and enforcing decisions would be simplified.

The state and federal governments already have control of the shallow coastal waters below low tide level, so that preservation of the shallow estuarine areas presents no great problem. It is, however, necessary to convince the agencies involved of the necessity of preserving these estuarine areas and to pass laws that will augment preservation. This will not be an easy task, but at least the difficulties of securing them from private ownership do not have to be overcome.

Most of the coastal marshes, however, are privately owned, even in those states which claim ownership up to high tide level. Either the marshes lie above what is officially called high tide or they may have been privately controlled for so long that the states have lost effective controls of them. These lands must be protected immediately from the actions of individual owners which would be harmful to the public at large.

Land next to the coast has increased so rapidly in value that it is under special pressure for development. In the not too distant future, it will be entirely built up, whether or not we use the salt marshes. If we insist on preserving the marshes now, the coastal land available for development will be gone only slightly sooner. We will have to find alternate solutions to the problem of coastal population expansion anyway. While there is still a maximum of choice, we must preserve what we can. Once the decision has been made to preserve a marsh area, regardless of its size, we must not give in to the pressures that always develop to try to reverse the decision.

There seems to be no reason why the construction of new marshland would be an impossibility. Perhaps in connection with the dredging of navigation channels or other destructive activities, the deposition of the dredging spoil could be made in such a way as to create intertidal flats which could then be planted with marsh grass. It might be possible to get a new marsh well established within only a few years if it were adequately planted. We know of no case in which this has been tried, but it is certainly worth some effort and experimentation.

The states along the Eastern seaboard have a variety of programs which could be used as good or bad examples of estuarine and marsh management. These include zoning provisions which attempt to restrict the use of marsh and estuarine lands to that which will not damage their value as conservation areas and flood control areas.

Regulatory laws are fairly common in which the state determines what dredging and filling may be done on state land by making it necessary for a developer to obtain a permit before proceeding with any action. In a few cases, permits are required, not only for state-owned land, but for private uplands and marshes bordering the estuaries as well.

In some states there are acquisition programs under way in which the state protects its marshland by actual purchase. Through the Bureau of Sports Fisheries and Wildlife, the federal government has protected considerable areas of salt marsh by including them in federal wildlife refuges. The state regulation and acquisition programs are best developed in the northeast and at the moment are almost nonexistent in the southeast, wherein lies the bulk of the productive marshes.

Maine has a law which requires a permit before public or private coastal wetlands may be altered. The law is designed to prevent damage to the fisheries value of the coast. There is also an acquisition program by the Fish and Game Department of the state which has acquired some of the Scarboro marsh. The Federal Bureau of Sports Fisheries and Wildlife is also acquiring three to four thousand acres of marshes along the southeast coast of Maine.

New Hampshire has a law requiring a permit to alter its marshes and has an acquisition program under the State Fish and Game Department which is off to a slow start but for which there is considerable hope. There is increasing local interest in the preservation of marshes. The Society for the Protection of New Hampshire Forests has been very active in promoting salt marsh preservation in the state.

Massachusetts has a Wetlands Permit Law which prohibits the removing or dredging of any bank, flat, or marsh meadow or swamp bordering on coastal waters without specified local and state permission. This permit law has been upheld in a court test. The ruling in this case contains the first legal reference to salt marshes as necessary to the preservation of fisheries. Massachusetts has another law which specifies a regulatory approach to the preservation of salt marshes. Under this law, the Commissioner of Natural Resources may adopt regulations or rules concerning alteration or pollution of marshes which apply to whole regions of the coast. This permits conservation plans to be designed and implemented before private development plans get to the permit request stage. This second law has not yet been tested in the courts. If the courts rule that the restrictions under either the permit law or the regulatory law constitute a taking of land without compensation, the Department of Natural Resources may proceed to condemn the land and take it by eminent domain. This means that the owner of the marsh will be given adequate compensation for his land and that the cost of preserving the lands will be borne by the public at large rather than by the individual owner.

Massachusetts also has a state law authorizing towns to establish Town Conservation Commissions. These local bodies are doing an excellent job of watching over marshes within the individual towns and encouraging their towns to acquire marshes for conservation purposes. Under this combination of approaches, the future of salt marshes in Massachusetts looks as bright as it does anywhere along the coast.

Rhode Island has a permit law regulating privately owned marshes as well as state-owned lands. This law has been interpreted rather strictly in the recent past and no filling has been permitted. In fact, two town dumps on marshes have been shut down. The Department of Natural Resources owns over four hundred acres or about twenty-five percent of the salt marshes in the state and hopes to acquire more when funds are available. Funds have come through a Green Acres Bond Issue which provides money for the Department of Natural Resources to acquire land, but without specific budgeting for salt marshes. The Department has no power to take land by condemnation.

The state of Connecticut does not have a permit law regulating filling of marshes from the landward side. The Water Resources Commission, however, has control over tidal waters and can control dredging and filling projects along the outer edges of salt marshes. Unfortunately, its conservation record is rather poor. The Fish and Game Board in Connecticut can acquire marshes by condemnation as well as by gift and purchase. It now owns over four thousand acres and would like to acquire some seven thousand more. There is hope that the remainder of the still existing Connecticut marshes will be acquired by towns and other conservation agencies.

New York has no specific estuarine controls. The Water Resources Commission can take land by eminent domain but the power has not been widely used for marsh preservation. The Long Island Wetlands Act permits cooperative agreement between towns in Long Island and the state to preserve marshes. A fifty/fifty sharing of the maintenance of these lands, between the state and local governments, is provided in the agreement. The town of Hempstead was the first to take advantage of this provision and now a total of fifteen thousand acres of the Long Island salt marshes has come under this type of agreement. There is hope that thirty-one thousand acres will eventually be included which will cover most of the existing high value marshes on Long Island. There is a big flaw in the plan. The agreements are subject to cancellation by either state or town and so carry no permanent safeguard.

New York passed a bond act in 1960 for park and recreation land acquisition but so far only two hundred acres of salt marsh have been acquired. Some salt marsh will be permanently protected in the Fire Island National Seashore. Other portions of salt marsh are owned by the Nature Conservancy, by Sportsmen's Gun Clubs or by conservation-oriented individuals. The last lands, as well as those held under the cooperative agreement between towns and state, will be subject to increasing pressure as taxes increase and further population pressures develop on Long Island. A more permanent form of protection is needed for these extremely important marshes.

New Jersey embarked on a large-scale acquisition effort as part of its sixty million dollar Green Acres Bond Issue voted by a large majority in 1964. The state, under this program, has acquired some twenty thousand acres of salt marsh and is in the process of getting fifty thousand more. Since the state previously owned thirty thousand acres, and the federal government owns about fifty thousand acres in wildlife refuges, the total protected area will be about one hundred and fifty thousand acres. This figure represents sixty-five percent of the salt marshes remaining along the New Jersey coast and ninety percent of the most valuable of those marshes.

In Delaware, about forty thousand of the one hundred and fifteen thousand acres of salt marshes are protected from development either as a result of ownership by the Delaware Fish and Game Commissioners or by being included in the Bombay Hook and Prime Hook National Wildlife Refuges. The state planning office has designated some marshes for conservation use, but it has no real power to prevent development. The remaining marshes are, therefore, highly vulnerable. Moreover, an accelerated mosquito ditching program, undertaken in 1965 and 1966, has reduced the value of these remaining marshes to waterfowl.

Maryland, again, provides for real protection of salt marshes only through state ownership. The state owns large shallow water areas, while the marshes are principally in private hands. There is an extensive planning study under way which demonstrates the concern of the Maryland government for the preservation of its marshes, but at the moment, the marshes are highly vulnerable to destruction.

Virginia protects none of its marshes except those owned outright by the state. The state is considering study plans for more action. One of the difficulties in

Virginia is a division of responsibility between various agencies, characteristic as well of other states which have no comprehensive plan of action. The Commission of Game and Inland Fisheries, the Commission of Fisheries, the Water Control Board, and the Division of Water Resources share the responsibilities for dealing with salt marshes.

North Carolina, at the moment of writing, is in a similar situation, but the State Interagency Council on Natural Resources appointed an estuarine study committee to develop a comprehensive state program for multiple use of the state's estuaries. This program is to be presented in time for implementation by the 1969 general assembly. The study committee has proposed that a centralized authority take over responsibility for the state's estuarine program and coordinate the efforts of the various agencies involved.

The committee has proposed that North Carolina acquire one hundred thousand to one hundred fifty thousand acres of salt marsh. The larger number would include nearly ninety percent of the high value marshes in the state. They further propose a permit system controlling use of the marshes and perhaps a regulatory law similar to that existing in Massachusetts. This suggested program, if adequately funded, is an excellent one and deserves to be enacted. It could serve as a model for similar programs in other southeastern states.

South Carolina has no specific legislation regulating the marshes and no acquistion program. It has only the usual fish and game laws, pollution laws, and permit requirement for dredging state lands. Some salt marsh areas are preserved by the state for waterfowl hunting. Another thirty thousand acres are preserved in the Cape Romain National Wildlife Refuge.

Georgia has no marsh acquisition program and imposes no regulation on the use of marshes. Most of those marshes that are preserved are located in federal wildlife refuges. The marshes surrounding Sapelo Island already belong to state agencies or are likely to be taken soon, as is the case with the marshes surrounding St. Catherine's Island. There is some interest in the creation of a national seashore on Cumberland Island which would preserve the marshes associated with that island as well.

The state of Florida has made a start in marsh and estuarine conservation by enacting the Bulkhead Law designating the line beyond which no filling is allowed. The bulkhead line is established at the local level and approved by the state. This is a good start but has obvious limitations. For example, there is no control over the source of the fill. Large areas of Florida marsh and mangrove swamp have been preserved in the Everglades National Park and forty thousand acres of marsh have been preserved in the Cape Kennedy National Wildlife Refuge. The state is also creating marine preserves, such as that in Estero Bay, in which a large area of red mangrove and turtle grass is preserved as a fisheries resource.

There is also a valuable example for other states to follow in the ruling by the Florida Board of Health in 1951, in which the use of any organic insecticides on salt marshes or other natural environments is outlawed. This ruling has probably been directly responsible for the fact that Florida's estuaries are less polluted by pesticides than those of almost any other state.

Progress is being made in the preservation of marshes and associated wetlands along the Atlantic coast. But so far only Massachusetts and New Jersey can be said to have reasonably adequate programs already under way. Even there, progress depends on continued adequate funding.

Two other areas might be mentioned, although they are outside the geographic limits of this book: one on the West Coast, and the other around the Gulf of Mexico. The state of California has undertaken an extensive planning program for estuarine conservation in the San Francisco Bay area. The Gulf States Marine Fisheries Commission has set up a committee, the Estuarine Technical Coordinating Committee, which is planning an extensive survey of the estuarine resources of the Gulf Coast to be made with all new data and completed by the summer of 1970. This concerns itself largely with the coast of Louisiana, which contains four to five million acres of coastal marsh and enclosed water, a much more extensive area than is found in any of the other Gulf Coast states.

A resource survey and a logical plan for development is obviously the first step which must be taken everywhere in the conservation of salt marshes and estuaries. Our coastline will soon, certainly within the lifetime of some now living, be almost entirely developed in one way or another. This development should include permanent conservation of considerable areas of estuaries and salt marsh. As in the case of mosquito control, we are able to look to Massachusetts for an example of a well thought out plan for marsh conservation. But even in Massachusetts, marshes are disappearing which ought to be preserved.

Direct purchase of the land by public conservation agencies is the most obvious and most certain solution. Unfortunately, direct purchase is the most expensive means of acquiring marshes. The more the pressure for development of a specific marsh, the more expensive it is and the greater the necessity for quick action. Purchase may well be the only way to save marshes that are under extreme pressure. But, even with the participation of the federal government, funds for the direct purchase of marshes are limited.

The Marine Resources Committee deserves mention for its efforts in preserving coastal habitats. Besides planning conservation and coordinating efforts of various groups, the Committee raises funds and purchases threatened wetlands. It holds these for eventual acquisition by federal, state, or private conservation agencies, thus providing stopgap funds to assure preservation.

Marshes that are less immediately threatened might possibly be saved by less expensive means. Restrictive zoning has been used but is probably not an effective means for preservation. The courts have found, in a number of instances, that use restriction can become tantamount to taking of land if the restrictions on the owner are too sweeping. If the public wants preservation, it should be willing to pay for it and not make the marsh owner bear its burden. But, although conservation zoning may be too restrictive and therefore unconstitutional, it should be possible for towns and states to zone the land by purchasing the rights to fill, build, dredge, or mine. The buying of easements might be particularly effective in marshes that are less immediately threatened. The owner would retain hunting and fishing rights and the right to prevent trespass but would sell to the locality or state the rights to alter the marsh in any way. This method would preserve the marsh's value as a food source and a nursery ground for estuarine animals and would leave it as a buffer against storm damage.

Whatever method is used to preserve marshes, it must include safeguards against the increased pressures to develop because of the ever increasing population. There have been too many cases in which the last land in the town, land reserved for park and playground, has been diverted to industrial use. The diversion occurred because the industry threatened to move to another town or even another state if it were not allowed to secure the land. This sort of corporate blackmail is hard to withstand and will inevitably bring pressures on organizations controlling the marshes.

Pressure even comes from the state officials who are trying to encourage industries to come to their area by offering filled marsh for building. The battle between the forces of development and conservation need be won only once by the developers but must be fought and won every year for conservation to triumph.

In the last hundred years, our nation has been called on to preserve certain unique natural resources such as those contained in many of our national parks: Grand Canyon, Yosemite Valley, the Yellowstone hot springs, Mammoth Cave, the Everglades, and the Cape Cod seashore. Now we are confronted with the problem of preserving a different sort of natural resource. This resource is much more extensive—the ribbon of green marshes along the eastern coast of North America, which must be preserved almost in its entirety if its preservation is to have any real meaning.

Index